OLD FAITHFUL
A History of Hull Football Club

1865 - 1987

WITH 1988 UPDATE

by
Michael E. Ulyatt

with
Rugby League Statistical Records by
Bill Dalton

and
Foreword by Lord Derby

HUTTON PRESS

1988

Published by the Hutton Press Ltd.
130 Canada Drive, Cherry Burton, Beverley
North Humberside HU17 7SB

Copyright © 1988

First published 1988
Reprinted with update 1989

Printed and Bound by

Clifford Ward & Co. (Bridlington) Ltd.
55 West Street, Bridlington, East Yorkshire
YO15 3DZ

ISBN 0 907033 63 6

To the Memory
of
Albert Saville

CONTENTS

FOREWORD BY THE PRESIDENT
OF THE RUGBY FOOTBALL LEAGUE

I am delighted to have the opportunity of writing the Foreword to this history of the Hull Football Club.
Founded in 1865, they joined the English Rugby Union in 1872 and are therefore one of the oldest Rugby Clubs in the North of England.
Hull were founder members of the Northern Union in 1895 and so they have had a long and proud association with Rugby League Football.
I wish them well in the years to come.

Rt. Hon. Earl of Derby, M.C.,
President of the Rugby Football League,
January 1988

ACKNOWLEDGEMENTS

It's nearly 40 years since Colin McCune and Cyril Smith first took me to the Boulevard. We caught the single-decker Fish Dock bus in Sculcoates Lane to the top of Albert Avenue and walked along Anlaby Road to the ground. Another route we would use was to catch a No. 63 trolley bus at Melwood Grove on Beverley Road to King Edward Street in the city centre and then onto a No. 69 trolley bus outside the City Hall and along Anlaby Road, getting off at St. Matthews Church at the top of the Boulevard. We paid our money at the turnstile and standing on the cinder shale, high up behind the goalposts at the Airlie Street end of the ground, it was a strange new world to me. Expressions like 'play yer ball, gerrem onside ref, 'it 'im 'ard Charlie, on the burst' were to become commonplace.

My most vivid memories are of Freddie Miller's end to end touchline kicking duels with the opposition's full back, the slick running of winger Bruce Ryan, the tigerish tackling of 'Ginger' Burnell and the solid grafting of Charlie Booth. Although soccer was my first love, I became fiercely proud of 'my rugby league team'.

I went to my first Rugby League Final in 1956 when my schoolpal Peter Blanchard and I travelled by steam train to Manchester and watched our favourites beat Halifax 10-9 in the Championship Final at Maine Road. It was to be 26 years before I saw Hull win another Final, the 1981/2 season when they won the John Player Trophy. It was well worth the wait!

A chance conversation with that grand sporting character Len Young in 'Percy Johnson's Royal Box' at the Corn Exchange Pub in the heart of Hull's Old Town sometime during the spring of 1987 led to my introduction to Bill Dalton and the idea of this book was born.

Since then, I am grateful to Max Gold for the loan of his scrapbook; to the Hull Daily Mail for permission to use photographs from their collection; to Dave and Alan Hall for all their help and advice; and to Malcolm Fussey for copying many of the old photographs.

I thank everyone who helped with information, however small, in my research, and to Maureen Foers, thanks for arranging the typing of my manuscript.

Many supporters of Hull F.C. have been more consistent fans than I, but we all have one thing in common - we want the club to prosper. Long may it do so.

Michael E. Ulyatt,
January 1988

My thanks go to Irvin Saxton and the Rugby League Record Keepers' Club for statistical confirmation; Chris Park for use of his excellent photographic collection; the Local Studies Library, Central Library Hull for access to their newspaper files; my good friend Chris Elton and the late Tom Webb for all their help with statistics.

Bill Dalton,
January 1988

THE EARLY YEARS

The Hull Football Club was formed in 1865 by a group of former public schoolboys, mainly from Marlborough, Cheltenham, Rugby and St. Peters', York. These included W.H.H. Hutchinson, B. Lambert, E. Waltham, R.J. Wade and the five Scott brothers - F.A. Scott, G. Cooper Scott, Henry Scott, Charles Scott and J. Scott. Their father was the Rev. John Scott, vicar of St. Mary's, Lowgate and he also helped to run a Rifle Volunteer group.

The club's first ground was at Woodgates Hall, North Ferriby, the home of the Harrisons, and although some difficulty was experienced in finding suitable opponents, games were arranged with Newark, Bramham College, Louth and St. Peter's, York. By 1870 they were playing Bradford, York, Leeds and Huddersfield but because of the distances which had to be travelled to Hull by steam train, the club's President, John Loft, rented a "ground" at Selby opposite the Londesborough Arms. This was roughly halfway between Hull and the "far" West Riding and the landlord did not charge a rent for the field, allowing his pub to be used as changing rooms for both teams. He probably gained from the sale of beer and food after the matches.

A meeting held in the George Hotel on October 10th 1870 decided "it was not lawful to take up the ball when it was rolling and no player should stand on the goal bar to interrupt its going over". Quite how a player climbed up there is not recorded! Each club had its own rules, usually unwritten and before the match the two captains would agree rules to be played under.

After 1871, a new ground was obtained, the Rifle Barracks field in Londesborough Street, Hull and in 1872 Hull became one of the first clubs in the North of England to join the English Rugby Union.

Members of the club around this time were the Hodgsons (William, Richard, Edward and Arthur), the Harrisons (Gilbert, Walter and Brian), F. Moss, E.W. Wade, Darbyshire, Norman and Salmon. In the first Yorkshire county match against Lancashire at Leeds, Hull had four members of the team, Waltham, Wood, Lambert and Hutchinson. The club's first colours were striped scarlet and white jersey, white cap (if any) and white flannels with the city's Three Crowns in a black badge on the jersey. Later, a move was made to a ground at the Haworth Arms field in Newland and when Huddersfield were the visitors, there were just twenty spectators! E.W. Wade kicked a late goal to give Hull victory. Both teams scored nine tries apiece.

Hull were now considered to be among the strongest sides in Yorkshire in 1877, and when the Yorkshire Challenge Cup was introduced in that year, they were favourites to win "t'owd tin pot", but York beat them in the semi-finals. Representative honours came to Hull when Gilbert Harrison was chosen to play for England seven times between 1877 and 1885. New members included J.H. Hodge (Secretary), W. Vassall and H.F. Lowe (from Cheltenham), E.T. Wise (Treasurer) and W.J. Tall (from Rugby), W.S. Beaumont (from St. Peter's, York) plus David Wilson, A. Thorney, Thompson, Brough, Plaxton, W.J. Close, A.W. Lambert, H. Tall, A. Smithson, A.H. Tyacke, J.L. Read, R.E. Denett, J.C. Shears, West, Joy, Bethell, H. Williams and W. Calvert. Only sixteen members were actively involved on the playing side, and great difficulty was met in raising teams for away fixtures.

HULL WHITE STAR F.C. SEASON 1879/1880

Back Row (l. to r.): C. A. Brewer (Hon. Treas.), E. M. Braithwaite, B. R. Wilson, G. G. Watson, W. Gibson, L. Whitehead, F. L. Mawer, C. H. Mawer, G. W. Braithwaite.
Middle Row: P. E. Dickinson, W. H. Ellis (President), S. Bell.
Front Row: J. Douglas, W. Close (Hon. Sec.), J. C. Lightowler, G. A. Hoskins (Capt.), T. Harrison, H. Roberts, T. Sparrow.

Ten matches were played, five won, two lost and three drawn. There were thirty playing members in season 1878/9 when nine matches were won, two lost and one drawn. Secretary H.F. Lowe announced "a team list can be viewed on Wednesday evening at the Imperial Hotel, Paragon Street" and "Club jerseys are available from Harland and Co. of Silver Street". Mr. Lowe's office was at 19 Parliament Street. Interest in rugby grew in 1879 and with forty-five playing members, a second team was formed. Thirteen first team matches were played, six won, four lost and three drawn. Hull were now playing on Anlaby Road, where West Park is now situated.

W.H.H. Hutchinson was born in Cottingham in 1849 and lived at Cottingham Hall. He attended Rugby school and played regularly in twenty-a-side games. He became a shipowner in Hull and remembered early matches for Hull: "Players unaware of the rules would grab my hair when I charged past them". In a match for Yorkshire against Lancashire, several Sheffield players "also with little knowledge of the rules, did not like the hard tackling of a Lancashire forward and one of the Sheffield men grabbed the ball by the lace and hammered his opponent about the head with it. I had to tell him it was not provided for in the rules and he seemed surprised to learn it!" Hutchinson played twice for England.

Hull lost twice to a junior club, Hull White Star, in the 1879/80 season and Hull's Secretary J.H. Hodge put a resolution to his members "that this club cease to exist, subject to the Hull White Star Club taking our name and our members without ballot", and at the same time, Hull White Star resolved to "change our name to Hull Football Club and to admit all members of the late Hull Football Club". Both clubs passed these resolutions.

Hull White Star's history started in 1873 when a rugby team called Albert

George A. Hoskins   *Fred L. Mawer*

played on Todd's Field on Sutton Bank as did a side named Zingari, whose members were mainly cricketers. They formed the White Star Cricket Club in the summer and in turn they formed the Hull White Star Football Club. The club's first Secretary was W.J. Close and Treasurer Charles Brewer, who was also a half back and topped the try scoring list one season. Mr. Brewer later became President of Hull F.C.

White Star played under association football rules with Lincolnshire clubs and rugby with a few Yorkshire teams. Their playing strip was firstly a blue and white jersey and later a black jersey with a white star emblazoned on the chest, black knickers and black stockings. They rented a ground on David Pearson's field, Sweet Dews Farm, behind the Anti-Mill on Holderness Road in 1875 and played matches against Gainsborough (celebrating afterwards at the White Hart, Gainsborough) and against Brigg (followed by a visit to The Angel Hotel, Brigg).Eleven matches were completed in 1877 including fixtures against Hull seconds, York Amateurs, Selby and Market Rasen. A new ground had been taken on Hall's Field, further along Holderness Road. The rent was £4.00 in the first season and Secretary W.J. Close recalled later that at the first club match when gate money was taken, it amounted to 2/6d and match expenses were 3/6d! Later gate receipts included 14/- v Brigg; £1/14- v Ossett; 9/3d v Stanley; 15/10d v Southgates; £2/6/- v Barnsley; 10/2d v Malton; £2/8/3d v Gainsborough; £4/15/4½ v Hull

11

and £3/8/2½ v York. The first West Riding club to be played was Kirkstall. Members around this time included P. Dickinson, G.W. Braithwaite, T. Sparrow, S. Bell, C. Lightowler, C.H. Mawer, F. Mawer, W.J. Close, T. Adams, J. Wilkins, G.A. Hoskins, C. Whitehead, T. Harrison, E.M. Braithwaite and F.R. Helman.

Thirteen matches were played in 1879, six were won, four lost, and three drawn. Gibson scored five tries, Lovell three goals and Wilson two goals. Over five hundred miles were travelled to six away matches and home gates of 500 were reported. A balance of £4/9/4d was announced. Club jerseys could be obtained from Maw Till Kirk Co. of Bridge Street.

On the fusion of the two clubs, new team colours were introduced, a black jersey with the Three Crowns emblem in blue and gold on the chest but later a change back to cherry and white stripes was made. However it was discovered that these two colours "ran" when washed and the club reverted back to black jerseys with white knickers, hence the nickname "The All-Blacks" in the late 1880's/early 1890's. The ground at Holderness Road (on land where Mersey and Severn Streets now stand) could hold 2,500 in two stands covered with a corrugated iron roof and 2,500 at the two ends. There was a four foot high fence around the playing area, large shields with coat of arms on the goal lines and the centre line. The 25 yard lines were marked with large shields and a large board on the front of one covered stand near its roof informed the crowd of the length of time over which the game was to be played. There were three turnstiles and admission was 3d. The "amalgamation" proved a real shot in the arm for rugby in Hull and the East Riding and membership on the playing side quickly grew to eighty-six. During the 1880 season eighteen matches were played: eight were won, six lost and four drawn. The first officers of the club were W. Ellis (President), G.A. Hoskins (Captain), Vice-Presidents, Dr. Holder, E. Atkin, G.W. Braithwaite, Treasurer, F. Tindle and Hon. Secretary W.J. Close. Matches were played in Yorkshire, Lancashire, Durham and Northumberland, and short tours of the U.K were undertaken. A sum of £2/8/5d was spent on advertising the change of name to those concerned with rugby union. Nine players had won their county caps - G. Jacketts, W. Calvert, G. Belt, F.L. Mawer, E. Coulman, H. Simpson, A.P. Iveson, W. Teal and H.J.W. Oxlade.

The club's A.G.M. of 1881/2 was held at the Nags Head Inn on Holderness Road and it revealed that there were now 133 members, with nine matches won and fourteen lost. Fixtures had been played with Scarborough, Dewsbury Shamrocks, Salterhebble, Leeds St. John, York Melbourne, Ossett, York St. Peters and Kirkstall among others. G.A. Hoskins was the leading try scorer with ten, and D.R. Lovell topped the goal kicking list. On October 8th, the team which played Scarborough away on the cricket field was: Lovell, Hoskins, Wilson, Smith, Smithson, Tyacke, Robinson, the Tall brothers, Beaumont, Braithwaite, Read, Winter, Close and Womack. Hull won by two goals to two tries, one try and eight touchdowns to one try and two touchdowns. The balance sheet recorded a season's gate money of £103.00 and £1/6/- spent on purchasing rugby balls. Nearly £41.00 went on travel by train to away matches. Sandwich board men had been used to advertise matches at a total cost of £3/12/6d! The Directors of the club recommended that the players kept fit in the summer months by playing the Canadian game of Lacrosse.

THE HULL FOOTBALL CLUB

Air - "A fine old English Gentleman".

We sometimes hear that Englishmen are going down the hill,
That in sport, and on the battlefield we've lost both nerve and will,
My song is of a mimic strife and deny it he who can,
That of the games of Britons, Rugby football leads the van.
CHORUS- Ho a jolly band of players, are the roving H.F.C.

In the Shire of broad acres, are many famous cracks,
From farfamed Wakefield Trinity, Bradford, Leeds and Halifax,
Bold Thornes, and many a plucky team descendant of John Bull,
But a Club to one day win the Cup, hails from the Town of Hull.
CHORUS- Ho a jolly band etc.

They fearlessly the pick of Yorkshire Football Clubs have faced,
Tho' often beaten in the field, have never been disgraced,
And of the men who've scored her well, I'll try to tell in rhyme,
I ask your patience till "no side" for now we've reached "half-time".
CHORUS- Ho a jolly band etc.

Will Calvert, Captain of the team, no courage does he lack.
Fleet of foot, and steady nerve, a sure three quarter back,
And next, a football pioneer, who's helped the Club to fame,
Here's a health to G.A. HOSKINS, football, and play the game.
CHORUS- Ho a jolly band etc.

The Brothers Braithwaite, George & Ted, have done their share of work,
And demon Smith, and sturdy Belt, were never known to shirk,
With Lovell stood between the posts, to kick the ball or run,
And the coming men are Smithsons, who with James will be A.1.
CHORUS- Ho a jolly band etc.

And now line up you forwards, just hear a word from me,
Close, Wilson, Winter and Lars Smith, with our reckless friend J.C.
And dashing Tyacke and Whitehead, you must all put archer up,
We'll give you hearty welcome with the Yorkshire Challenge Cup.
CHORUS- Ho a jolly band etc.

————————————

PRICE: ONE PENNY

A song sheet issued around this time

13

George Jacketts

W. F. B. Calvert

W. Teal

14

Hull F.C. Season 1881 - 1882
Back Row (l. to r.):L. Whitehead, H. L. Smith, G. W. Braithwaite, D. R. Lovell,
F. Winter, J. Wilson, F. Jones, A. H. Tyacke, E. Robinson.
Middle Row: W. Close; G. A. Hoskins (Capt.); W. F. B. Calvert.
In Front: L. A. Smith, A. Smithson, J. F. B. Calvert, E. M. Braithwaite.

By 1882 the club was really thriving and seventy members were recruited, giving a total membership of 205. Braithwaite, Hewetson and Co. erected a stand, boarded in and fenced round for £131/17/9d. Receipts included £308.00 taken in gate money and £11.00 rent received for grazing rights on the field! The average home gate was 3,000 while for the away match against Thornes, horses and rullies (carts) were hired to transport the team and officials at a cost of 8/6d. Lt. Col. Smith of Tranby Lodge, Hessle presided over the club's A.G.M., held at the Hull Temperance Club in Albion Street, and among players who received special mention were G. Braithwaite, J. Calvert and W. Calvert, F. Mawer, G. Hoskins and W. Tomlinson. Twenty-seven matches were played, eleven won, thirteen lost and three drawn. G.A. Hoskins scored seven tries and W. Tomlinson kicked six goals in his twenty-six appearances. It seemed that some members of the original Hull Club were conspicuous by their absence at the new club and they had preferred to "join junior clubs in the area". Over 1,700 miles were travelled to matches, including a short tour of the South of England in March. Seventeen members went and they received 30/- allowance and had their rail fares paid less 1/-, but they had to pay 5/- bed and breakfast per day themselves. The referee for the match against the Falcons at the Half Moon ground, Putney was Rowland Hill, Hon. Sec, of the Rugby Football Union and Hull won by two tries to nil. After the match "songs and recitations" were enjoyed after dinner at the Holborn

Restaurant, High Holborn. After a day's rest, Clapham Rovers were the opposition at Wandsworth Common and the Yorkshiremen were victors again, this time by one goal, two tries and three minor points to four minor points.

In the away match against Goole earlier in the season, their opponents disputed one of the referee's decisions and walked off the field of play, causing the match to be abandoned.

W.J. Close resigned as Secretary in 1883 after five years of service and at a dinner held in his honour at the Cross Keys Hotel, Market Place, he was presented with a solid silver tea and coffee service manufactured by Barnett and Scott of Hull. Mr. W. Hoskins, organist at St. James' Church, accompanied members on the piano. Fred Mawer was elected Secretary in his place and the club Captain was W.F.B. Calvert. Thirty-one matches were played, twelve won, fifteen lost and four drawn. The "Hull Times" instigated a Hull and district Rugby Union competition with a silver challenge trophy but the Hull first team was barred from entering to "equalise competition".

Three train loads of supporters followed the club to the Leeds St. John ground when Hull met Bradford in the Yorkshire Challenge Cup Final before a grand crowd of 15,000. Shortly before the kick-off, the Wellington Street area near to the ground was full of waggonettes, cabs and omnibuses but the match itself was a disappointment to the Hull fans. Their team's forwards played it tight but the backs were poor and Hull went down by one try to Bradford's four tries and one goal. Hull's team was:- W. Tomlinson, G. Calvert, J. James, B. Wilson, G. Belt, H. Bell, W. Calvert (capt.), G. Harrison, C. Simpson, G. Jacketts, J. Wilson, J. Calvert, F. Mawer, W. Teal and L. Whitehead. Fixtures during the season were arranged with Thornes, Manningham, Cleckheaton, Bingley and Horbury, among others. Larger crowds were being attracted and so a second grandstand was built to accommodate them and extensive work was carried out on pitch drainage. The yearly playing subscription was 5/-. Gilbert Harrison played for Yorkshire against Durham and Northumberland, and W. Calvert for Yorkshire against Cheshire and Oxford. A balance of £83/8/5d was reported and one item from the balance sheet was £16/6/- paid for referees' fees.

The club Chairman in 1884 was Mr. F. Tindle, and Fred Mawer and Doug Boyd were joint Secretaries. Yorkshire County honours came to F. Mawer, G. Belt, G. Harrison, W. Calvert and G. Jacketts. The club's membership was now three hundred and twenty and three new turnstiles were constructed to cope with increasing crowds. Thirty-four matches were played and nineteen were won, twelve lost and three drawn. H. Bell was an ever-present, W. Calvert and W. Teal were top try scorers and G. Jacketts was the leading goal kicker. The club's A.G.M. was held at the Queens Hotel and members heard details of the short tours of Lancashire and South Wales. Hire of buses from E.S. Annison during the season amounted to £19/8/6d and a balance of £363 was announced.

Bradford were unhappy at the injury to a player called Hawcridge and refused to renew their fixture with Hull the next season "because of the general rough and unscientific play of the Hull club".

Fixtures in 1885 included matches against Gala Melrose (Scotland), Swansea, Hartlepool, Sheffield, Horbury and Llanelli. W. Calvert was top try scorer with B.R. Wilson main goalkicker. Gilbert Harrison was selected as captain of York-

Bradford's Bonsor takes on Hull in the 1883 Yorkshire Cup Final at Leeds.

shire and E. Coulman and A.P. Iveson also played for their county. President Lt. Col. Smith (late Scots Guards) told the club's A.G.M. at the Public Rooms, Jarrett Street that membership stood at four hundred and sixty-eight and more construction work had to be carried out on the grandstand. Sickness benefit of £1/10/- was payable to players unable to work through injuries sustained playing rugby.

Halifax Cricket and Football Club invited Hull to play the first rugby match on their new enclosure in September 1886. G. Harrison and W. Teal played for Yorkshire and Hull's playing record was fifteen wins, eleven defeats and four draws. W. Calvert (tries) and W. Kassell (goals) topped the scorers' list and Calvert and F. Dickinson played in every match. Club caps were awarded to players after they had played thirty-five first team matches. The A.G.M., at the Gladstone Hall, Bond Street, heard of athletic sports held at the ground during the summer. The "A" team won the Hull and district Rugby Union Cup. J.C. Lightowler resigned as groundsman and J. Edson, former groundsman of Hull Town Cricket Club, replaced him. His wages were £63 for the season. The twelve acres of land which Hull rented at Holderness Road belonged to a Mr. Liddell, but as the tenure was due to be renewed the club looked at other options. One was extensive land at Hull Botanic Gardens at Spring Bank when the company running the Gardens went into liquidation. However, despite lengthy negotiations to purchase the land and talk of joining up with Hull Cricket Club, who planned to move from their Asylum Lane ground, the asking price proved too high and Hull Corporation eventually sold the land to the founders of Hymers College. During the season over 2,600 miles were travelled to fulfill fixtures including tours to London, Cambridge and Ireland where they met defeat on a tour for the first time, against Dublin University. That year's playing record was thirty-seven matches played, twenty-one won, eleven lost and five drawn. G. Harrison played for Yorkshire and so did H. Simpson, who was also the club's top try scorer in the season with twelve. G. Jacketts kicked most goals. Venues for the club's A.G.M's were certainly varied— that year's was held at the Central Hall, Pryme Street.

17

It was proposed in 1888 that the club should revert back to all black jerseys but this was defeated and the cherry and white strip survived for a short time. Gilbert Harrison's benefit brought him £31. Gate receipts in the season totalled nearly £1900 and one item of expenditure was £25 for the use of Turkish Baths. A.C. Bearmark and G. Jacketts were both selected for Yorkshire and Hull's two matches against the 'Maoris' brought in gate receipts of £458. The top try scorer was W. Calvert and most goals were kicked by A. Kilburn.

Hull's lease on their ground expired in 1889. The Southcoates Club had become virtually a nursery club for Hull while other local junior clubs who provided players included Marlborough, Three Crowns, Stepney Athletics, Holderness Wanderers, Stoneferry and Beverley. A. Iveson and T. Brennan headed the try scorers list and H. Thompson was "a champion goal kicker, top of the season's list". A Mr. Stuart of Waterworks Street was thanked in the annual report "for once again providing pineapples for the players". The season's playing record was fourteen wins, seventeen defeats and five draws.

The club's headquarters in 1890 were at the Queen's Hotel in Charlotte Street where William Teal was the proprietor. Wm. F.B. Calvert was 'mine host' at the Plimsoll Hotel in Witham, George Hoskins had a plumbing and gasfitting business in Wilton Terrace and Church Lane, and Fred Mawer ran a sports outfitting business in Witham. The club's official colours were changed back to all-black. During the season 65,556 adults and 6,330 juniors paid for admission. Thirty-four matches were played and fifteen were won, sixteen lost and three drawn. Top try scorer was J.W. Anderson and J. Sparviere kicked the most goals. William Herbert Wiles was signed from local club Marlborough, where he had been club captain. He began his playing career with St. Georges at the age of 14.

Gilbert Harrison was Club President in 1891 when a loss of £145/1/8d was announced. Thirty-five matches were played and fifteen were won, seventeen lost and three drawn.

Patrons of the club included Evans Fraser, F.R.C.S., F.B. Grotrian, M.P., H.S. King, M.P., C.H. Wilson, M.P., and Sir A.K. Rollit, M.P. New dressing rooms were built at the ground and J. Mather of 136 Wincolmlee advertised himself as "official sole contractor for boots for Hull F.C." A. Shillito with seven tries was top of the scores list and J. Sparviere topped the goal kickers list for the second successive season.

The President of the club in 1892 was W.J. Close and the club Captain was L. Donkin. The Mona club from the Isle of Man were hosted and the club's directors signed a renewal lease on the ground, thereby squashing strong rumours of a move to new headquarters. The season's playing record was twenty wins, fourteen defeats and three draws.

Hull were drafted into the Yorkshire Senior Competition in 1893 but finished a disappointing 10th out of 12 clubs. Fred Mawer resigned as club Secretary and G.W. Stephenson joined H. Hildreth as joint Hon. Secretary. The Hull Gymnastic Society offered the rugby club the use of their facilities for training purposes, an offer which was gratefully accepted. The services of the local police cost £14 during the season. Over 95,000 paid for admission at home matches. Will Mansell was top try scorer with six.

8th February 1893

HULL 7 V **HECKMONDWIKE 7**

WALT MANSELL	KNOWLES
W. JOHNSON	OATES
C. JEFFRIES 1 GOAL	ELLIS
J. TIMSON	JONES 1 TRY
C.H. TULLOCK	CLOUGH
A. LARARD 1 TRY	G. HARRISON
A. McKAY 1 TRY	JOWETT 1 TRY: 1 GOAL
L. DONKIN	S. HARRISON
A.C. BEARPARK	WALFORD
J. HOLMES	HARLAND
H.G. WATERS	ROBERTSON
R. ROBERTS	HALLIDAY
T. MARSDEN	ACKROYD
F. HARRISON	WELSH
C. RHODES	(only 14 played)

HALF TIME 2-2   Attendance:8,000

This game was played under "Electric Light" - without doubt Hull's first ever floodlit game. The "Hull Daily Mail" account states that 8 arc lamps each of 1000 candle power were set up and the generator for the lamps was powered by a Priestman Oil Engine situated under the West Stand. "The spectators in the East and West stands were able to obtain a good view".

A tour of the Lake District was undertaken in 1894. The Trippett Baths in Wincolmlee were hired from Hull Corporation Council for £23 and used for changing and washing accommodation. The Club's directors laid the basis for a momentous decision when they entered into negotiations for a ten year lease of the Athletic Grounds, near the Boulevard, at a rent of £150 a year. Their tenure of the Holderness Road ground was uncertain but after signing a lease for the Athletic grounds, the directors changed their minds and decided to stay in the east of the city. However the directors of the Athletic Grounds held them to their contract. A scheme to lease the two grounds never really got off the ground and the Holderness Road venue was sold off for building land. Hull Kingston Rovers had been

C. C. Lempriere

playing at the Athletic Grounds and they moved across the River Hull to a ground in Craven Street off Holderness Road. Hull finished 11th out of the 12 clubs and had the remarkable record of not scoring in 12 of their 22 league matches. Cyril C. Lempriere had the distinction of captaining the club during their last full season at Holderness Road and the first one at the Athletic Grounds. Nicknamed 'Lemp', he was a wing threequarter and made his club debut in 1892, scoring 5 tries in 26 matches. He began playing rugby with Radley College in 1886 and then played with Worcester College, Oxford between 1889 and 1892 and occasionally turned out for Oxford University. At this time Gilbert Harrison died. Born at Cottingham, he was an early stalwart of the club. Off the field he was a partner in Harrison Brothers, corn merchants, in High Street. £25 was donated to wives and children suffering through the Hull dock strike, as many of the club's fans worked on the docks.

It was a time of real change for club and country - a new government, location and constitution.

A CHANGE OF DIRECTION

Hull severed membership with the Yorkshire and England Rugby Unions and entered the Northern Rugby Union as founder members together with Manningham, Halifax, Runcorn, Oldham, Brighouse Rangers, Tyldesley, Hunslet, Leigh, Wigan, Bradford, Leeds, Rochdale Hornets, Warrington, St. Helens, Liversedge, Widnes, Stockport, Batley, Wakefield Trinity, Huddersfield and Broughton Rangers. After the inaugural meeting at the George Hotel, Huddersfield on 29th August, 1895, Hull's directors were empowered to pay playing members for *bona fide* broken time, i.e. payment could be made for players having to take unpaid time off work to play rugby. £195 was paid by the club for 'broken time' during the season. Gates increased and a record crowd of 15,000 watched the home match against Bradford on Good Friday.

Their first match to be played in the Northern Union was away to Batley on September 7th, when Hull went down 3-7, Holmes scoring the try. The team was: Johnson, Lempriere, Jacques, J. Townend, Duncan Wright, C. Townend, G. Barker, Mansell, Booth, Feetham, Holmes, Harmer, Carr, F. Spenceley, G. Jacketts.

The first home match was against Liversedge on 21st September, when a try from Jacketts gave Hull a 3-0 victory. Finishing 8th out of 22 (there was no cup competition), the full season's playing record was played 42, won 23, lost 16. Three matches were drawn, with 259 points for and 158 against. £2,725 was taken on the gate in the 22 home matches and a profit of £485 was made on the season. A loss of £608 was made on the sale of the club's old property on Holderness Road. A total of 3,260 miles was travelled to matches. Two new stands were erected, the east stand having dressing room accommodation under it.

The opposition failed to score in 14 of the matches and L. Donkin became the club's first Northern Union County player when he was selected for Yorkshire v Lancashire. Members of the press expressed a wish for a telegraph box to be erected. W. Mansell was ever present, and again in 1896 when Charlie Townend was club Captain. Charles had developed his rugby skills at West Hartlepool R.U. club under the expert tuition of Sammy and Jack Morfitt and he was described as "the finest man in the north of England to have behind a scrummage". J. Porter became joint Hon. Secretary and the popularity of membership of the Northern Rugby Union became even more apparent with crowds still growing. The press asked for their seats to be moved from the south end of the east stand nearer the centre of that stand. Local charities still benefitted from the agreement that proceeds of the match on Hull Fair Day in October be donated to them.

Hull finished 11th in the League the next season when the average home gate was 7,016 and a new record crowd of 15,500 watched the home match against Bradford. Under the captaincy of C.C. Lempriere, the playing record was 40 matches played, 18 won, 17 lost and 5 drawn. 41 goals and 72 tries were scored (298 points) with 35 goals and 53 tries against (229 points). J.W. Smith (tries) and Billy Jacques (goals) topped the scorers' list and T. Savage played in 38 of the matches. The 'A' team had a most successful season, winning the Junior Eastern Competition and then beating Bradford, winners of the Western Competition, by 10 points to 3. Their top scorers in the season were R. Sanderson (62 goals) and G.

First team to play for Hull at The Boulevard, v Liversedge, September 21st, 1895
Back Row (l. to r.): H. Hildreth (Hon. Joint Sec.), C. A. Brewer (President), G. Jacketts,
G. W. Stephenson (Hon. Joint Sec.)
Third Row: H. Wiles, W. Mansell, W. Harmer, J. S. Barker, J. Townend, G. Booth, J. Gray
(Attendant).
Second Row: E. Mahoney, H. Thompson, C. C. Lempriere (Captain), C. Townend, W. Johnson,
A. Plugge.
Front Row: G. E. Barker, W. Feetham, J. Holmes.

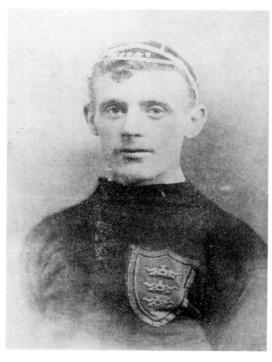

Charlie Townend

C.H. Brewer, President 1898

Jack Townend, Vice-Captain 1898

William Herbert Wiles, Captain in 1898

William Jacques

1898/9
Back Row (l. to r.): H. Hildreth (Hon. Sec.), F. Gorman, R. Rhodes, C. A. Brewer
(President), H. Wiles, F. Cornish, J. Townend, J. Gray (Attendant),
Second Row: W. Jacques, P. Fildes, G. Voyce, J. Thompson (Captain), W. Dale, R. Parkinson,
L. Clubley (Hon. Treasurer).
Front: J. Driscoll, J. Tanner, W. Taylor, T. Savage, D. Franks

Barker (13 tries) and their average home gate was an astonishing 2,185. The 'A' team won the Eastern Division again in 1898 while the first team recorded a 86-0 victory over Elland in the first round of the Northern Union Cup, still a club record win. Jack Townend was Vice-Captain to W.H. Wiles. A popular player, Jack came to prominence with the White Star Club along with his brother Charlie, Billy Feetham, George Fletcher and Charlie Savage before he left to join West Hartlepool, and then came to Hull. A half back or threequarter, he was also a fine cyclist. The leading scorers were Cyril Lempriere (24 tries) and "Hockey" Driscoll (17 tries) while Billy Jacques kicked most goals and scored 169 points in all, topping the League's point scorers' list. Billy was Landlord at the Bangor Castle, Providence Row where junior club Westbourne had their headquarters.

Hull finished runners-up in the League and they had a great record of "nilling" the opposition 11 times out of 18 home matches and 17 times out of 34 in all matches played in the League and the N.U. Cup. The policy of giving each shareholder a season pass was continued.

The purchase of the Athletic Grounds was completed for £6,500 in 1899 and the ground was re-named the Boulevard. £125 rental was received for letting the ground to the "Savage South African Company Exhibition". New entrances to the ground were planned in the soon-to-be completed Airlie Street. A special match between East and West Yorkshire raised £118 for the Transvaal War Fund. It was the first season league matches were played against Hull Kingston Rovers' first team and although both matches were lost, the Hull F.C. Directors expressed a wish that "the good feelings between our two clubs will continue". Over 15,500 paid £514 to see the local derby match at the Boulevard.

Committee man Harry Dannatt was also mine host at the Shipping Office Hotel in Posterngate and he advertised "matches replayed every Sunday".

The Airlie Birds, as the club had been nicknamed, held their 1900 A.G.M. at St. Georges Hall in Story Street, when it was reported that former players F.L. Mawer, J. McKay and J. Galbraith had died during the year. The closure of the Earle's Shipyard on Hedon Road with the subsequent loss of jobs was held responsible for the drop of 462 subscribers to the club. Two points were deducted from their league total for playing J. Tanner in contravention of the rules, which stated a player should work on a Friday and the Saturday morning prior to a match.

The 37th annual report of the club in 1901 announced a new Chairman, Mr. F. Tindle and a new Hon. Secretary, S.H. Nicholls. T. Stitt captained the side to 11 wins, 13 defeats and 2 draws and a position of 8th out of 14 clubs was achieved in a year when a new Northern League was formed to obtain a higher standard of football. There was a faction in the club who actually wanted to return to rugby union football but this never became a strong possibility.

In 1902 Mr. E.C. Simpson was appointed Club Chairman. The death was announced of C.A. Brewer, who had looked after the interests of the club for so many years. The 'A' team won the Yorkshire Rugby Competition and beat Thrum Hall 73-0 to create a Combination League record score. A loss of £473 was reported on the year. General dissatisfaction was noted with the touch play rule and the playing the ball out of touch.

There was yet another change of Chairman in 1903 when W. Pool junior was elected at the club's A.G.M., held in the Albion Lecture Hall, Baker Street. H. Taylor was club Captain in a year when fully-representative teams could not be turned out regularly due to the working class rule and the club's directors voiced their opinion that open professionalism would be far better. Mr. A. Charlesworth of Dewsbury began a long association with the club when he was appointed Secretary at a salary of £151 per annum. Jack Harrison played in every match while an unfortunate accident happened to A. Moxon in the game against Runcorn when he injured a finger and it had to be amputated. £5 was collected for him on the ground. The 'A' team won the Yorkshire Junior Cup. Around this time, the club changed colours once again, this time to blue and white hoops.

The following season agreement was reached by Chairman Mr. W.F.B. Eyre with the directors of Hull City A.F.C. for them to use the Boulevard for three years on alternate Saturdays. J. Ritson was Club Captain and a benefit match for D. Frank raised £70. The authorities closed the Boulevard for two matches after the referee and the Hunslet team had been attacked by some of the crowd after a Challenge Cup Match. The game against Swinton was played at Beverley and the Hunslet league fixture took place at York's ground. Dr. G.W. Lilley provided medical services for the club and the 'A' team played against junior clubs only in Hull district, due to financial restrictions.

Harry Dannatt, Director

1901/2
*Back Row (l. to r.): J. H. Dannatt (Director), J. W. Tait (Director), Tom Coates
(Groundsman), L. Whitehead (Director), W. Pool (Director), W. Wright (Trainer)
Standing: C. Hunter (Trainer), S. H. Nicholls (Secretary), J. Ritson, F. Miller, A. Hambrecht,
H. Fulton, F. J. Bell, J. Wheeler, F. Tindle (President)
Seated: Billy Jacques, J. T. Thompson, F. Spenceley, T. Stitt (Captain), J. Wade, R. Parkinson,
H. Taylor
In Front: J. "Hockey" Driscoll, L. Parry, Dimmy Franks.*

26

1904/05

Standing (l. to r.): A. Charlesworth (Sec.), G Kilburn, R. Rhodes, J. Harrison, W. Langhorn, H. Fulton, J. Major, T. Coates (Groundsman).
Sitting: J. Ritson, J. Lewis, J. Cook, W. H. Taylor (Captain), J. Hufton, A. E. Freear, J. Wade, W. Mansell (Trainer).
Front Row: R. Goddard, F. Goodfellow, G. Hall, J. W. Burchell.

A League of 31 clubs was brought in for 1905 but Club Chairman Mr. J.H. Dannatt and his Board of Directors thought that a reconstructed league was a failure and standards throughout the season were low. The club finished 17th. An agreement was made with Hull Kingston Rovers to pool the two derby game receipts for the next couple of years.

The Hull Royal Infirmary, Sculcoates Dispensary, Victoria Childrens Hospital and Newland Orphan Homes were once again allowed to organise collections at the ground. A case of pipes was presented to L. Whitehead to mark his 25 years service to the club. A. Freear played for Other Nationalities against England. The club's top scorer was L. Parry with 19 tries. The Yorkshire Cup was instigated and Hull beat Bramley 5-2 in the first round before going down to Halifax 0-10 in the second round.

THE FIRST SUCCESSFUL YEARS

Ned Rogers signed on from local football in 1906 and went on to make a club record of 501 appearances. H. Wallace joined from West Hartlepool and was a season's ever-present.

P. Carvill was also an ever-present and scored 101 points with 21 tries and 19 goals. Liverpool City were beaten 63-2 in the first round of the Challenge Cup. Harry Taylor's benefit brought him £159 and the following year he captained Hull, Yorkshire and England sides. T. Herridge and J. Major played for Yorkshire, H. Wallace for Yorkshire and England while W. Holder won two international caps.

Congratulations were given at the club's A.G.M. held in Oddfellows Hall, Charlotte Street. The New Zealand tourists won 18-13 at the Boulevard in what was regarded as the best club game of the tour. Hull reached the final of the Northern Union Cup for the first time, beating Swinton, Salford, Wakefield Trinity and Leigh, but they went down 0-14 to Hunslet at Fartown, Huddersfield. The Club Chairman was J.F.H. Osborne and the Captain was W.H. Taylor. E. Rogers was top try scorer with 19.

The Australian tourists were beaten 9-8 in 1908 and after the tour, Jimmy Deveraux and Andy Morton became the first two 'Colonials' to sign for the club. Another important signing was Frank Boylen from Hartlepool Rovers R.U. and he played for the Northern Union in the Test Series against Australia. For the second season in succession, the Final of the Northern Union Cup was reached with victories over Normanton, Runcorn, Oldham and Halifax, with every match away from home. However, Wakefield Trinity won the Cup 17-0 at Headingley.

E. Rogers kicked 44 place goals and scored 17 tries during the season. The open East Stand at the Boulevard was re-built. About this time the club adopted the now famous black and white hooped jersey.

There was yet another successful cup run for the Boulevarders in 1909 when they reached the final of the Northern Union Cup for a record third successive time. Leigh, Batley, Halifax and Salford were defeated but after a 7-7 draw against Leeds at Huddersfield (which many thought Hull were extremely unlucky not to win) they went down 12-26 in the replay, again at Huddersfield. An exhibition match was played against St. Helens at Coventry, Hull winning 33-21 and the match itself was directly responsible for the formation of a new club in the Midlands. Chairman Mr. A.J. Boynton reported a profit of £198 on the year. W. Anderson was captain and Frank Boylen was selected for the Northern Union touring party to Australia and New Zealand. Jimmy Deveraux had a magnificent season scoring 21 tries while Edward Rogers kicked 61 goals and ran in 19 tries, a total of 179 points. Deveraux had an unlucky start to the 1910 season when he sustained a knee injury playing for the Colonials against the Returned Tourists at Headingley and he missed 18 matches. Alf Francis joined the club from Treherbert and set a club record of 27 tries. A further signing was E. Clarkson from Leigh. G. Connell was first team Captain and Ed Rogers had another fine season with 48 goals and 21 tries, a total of 159 points. The 'A' team won the East Riding League and the W.F.B. Eyre Cup. They also played an exhibition match against Hull Kingston Rovers 'A' team at Grimsby which brought in receipts of £50. The cycle

Ned Rogers

Tom Herridge

Frank Boylen (Forward)
Member of 1910 Tour Team to Australia

Harry Taylor

1907
*Back Row (l. to r.): A. Boynton, E. Fryall, G. Robinson, G. Miller, L. Whitehead, J. Osborne
(Chairman), A. Mennell, F. Foster, J. Pickering (all Directors).
Middle Row: W. Pool (Director), T. Herridge, W. Holder, J. Owen, J. Major, H. Fulton,
W. Lyon (Director), W. Eyre (Director), J. Dannatt (Director).
Front Row: H. Coates (Trainer), A. Charlesworth (Secretary), G. Cottrell, J. Castles,
E. Rogers, W.H. Taylor (Captain), G. Kilburn, T. Bruce, H. Wallace, W. Anderson.*

and running tracks at the Boulevard received special maintenance attention and a 20 mile race organised by the Amateur Athletic Union finished at the ground after the match against Coventry. Club programme sales amounted to over £6. The Earl of Derby agreed to become the President of the Northern Rugby Union.

Hull finished 10th in 1911 with a playing record of 20 wins, 15 defeats and 3 draws. They lost to the Australian tourists 7-26.

C.C. Lempriere presented Alf Francis with a gold medal to mark his club record try scoring feat during the previous season. "Mr. Reliable", Ed Rogers, was an ever-present and recorded 174 points with 72 goals and 10 tries. Ellis Clarkson received his International Cap and new signings in 1912 included a master stroke. Billy Batten joined the club from Hunslet at the end of the season for a massive fee of £600. Billy was well-paid but gave the club grand service. Earlier in the season Australian Herbert Gilbert was signed for a record Northern Union fee of £450. Herb was a born leader and was recognised as one of the fastest centres ever. He played for Souths, Wests and St. George and later became coach to St. George. Further Australians to come to West Hull that season were S.J. Darmody and W.R. Cappleman. Not surprisingly, players expenses rose to £2481 during the season but the average home gate jumped to 6,385. For the first time ever, the final

1909/10
Back Row (l. to r.): Whitehead, Porter, Mennell, Pickering, Miller, Osborne, Stevenson.
Next Row: Lewis (Trainer), Dannatt, Fulton, Holder, Walton, Herridge, Havelock, Cottrell,
Padgett, Dechan.
Sitting: Devereux, Rogers, Taylor, Anderson (Captain), Connell, Morton, Boylen, Wright
(Asst. Trainer).
Front Row: Rogers, Wallace (Vice-Captain).

of the Yorkshire Cup was reached and Hull beat Dewsbury, Halifax and Hunslet at home before going down 3-17 to Batley at Headingley. Yet another Cup Final lost! Ed Rogers kicked 50 goals and scored 4 tries to total 112 points and the club's top try scorer was Jack Harrison with 17. The 'A' team joined the Northern Rugby Combination.

What a season 1913/14 was for the Black and Whites, probably the most successful in the club's history. They finished fourth in the League, winning 24 matches out of 34 but lost to Huddersfield 5-23 in the semi-final of the Championship play-off. Club Captain Bert Gilbert became the first Colonial player to receive the Challenge Cup when first Salford, then Featherstone Rovers, Halifax and Huddersfield were beaten and then tries from Harrison and Francis gave Hull a 6-0 victory over Wakefield Trinity in the Final at Halifax. Many congratulations were received at the club, that they had won the Cup at last and a civic reception was held for players and officials at Hull City Hall. Jimmy Deveraux had returned to the club after a year's absence. Jack Harrison scored 23 tries during the season and Ed Rogers received a gold watch to mark his 1,000 points for the club and he once again reached a century of points during the season. Welsh International Alf

31

Jimmy Devereux

Alf Francis

Billy Batten

Bert Gilbert

Steve Darmody

1912
Standing (l. to r.): W. Wright (Asst. Trainer), G. Connell, G. Rogers, G. Cottrell. J. Major,
W. Holder, H. Havelock, G. M. Stevenson, J. Devereux, J. Lewis (Trainer).
Sitting: E. Atkinson, A. D. Morton, F. Boylen, W. H. Taylor (Captain), E. Rogers, H. Walton.
Front Row: H. Wallace, W. Anderson.

34

NORTHERN UNION CUP FINALIST 1914
Top: Ned Rogers
Second Row: (l. to r.): Bert Gilbert (Captain), Billie Batten.
Third Row: (l.) Alf Francis, (r.) Jack Harrison.
Fourth Row: Billie Anderson, Jimmy Devereux.
Fifth Row: Tom Milner, Greg Rogers.
Sixth Row: Dick Taylor, Billie Holder.
Seventh Row: Alf Grice, Tom Herridge, Steve Darmody.
Eighth Row: Sid Melville (Trainer), Mr. Charlesworth.
Ninth Row: Tim Allen, Joe Hammill, Percy Oldham.

35

Jack Harrison, VC, MC.

Francis was selected to tour Australia. A profit of £228 was made on the year and record gate receipts of £659 were announced at the home match against Hull Kingston Rovers.

It was the club's Golden Jubilee in 1914 and the A.G.M. heard that "the Great War on the Continent reduced gate receipts dramatically and strict economies are necessary", but, despite this exhortation, heavy losses were made on the season. Sid Deane joined the club from Australia and Jack Harrison was an ever-present, scoring a staggering 52 tries, still a club record. 770 points were registered, another club record. Rogers kicked 100 goals and Jimmy Deveraux touched down 21 times while Bert Gilbert also scored 21 tries before returning home to Sydney. Twenty-four players joined His Majesty's Forces and this contributed to a 31-0 defeat by Huddersfield in the Yorkshire Cup Final held at Headingley. The East Stand was extended and 405 numbered and reserved tip-up chairs were introduced. Bradford Northern were thrashed 65-0.

The great Billy Batten was elected Captain in 1915 when only "friendly matches" were played with no payments made to players. An unofficial league placed Hull third out of twenty-four teams. Guest players had to be used and a combined

***STEVE DARMODY'S BENEFIT MATCH, EAST RIDING v WEST RIDING,
6th MAY 1916 AT THE BOULEVARD***

*West Riding - Standing (l. to r.): G. Rees (Leeds), J. Beasty (Hull), J. E. Wyburn (Hull),
W. Fowler (Hunslet), J. W. Higson (Huddersfield), Jack Donaldson (Australian sprinter),
W. Wagstaff (Huddersfield), Steve Darmody, H. Buck (Hunslet), E. Batten (Hull), W. Jukes
(Hunslet).*
*Kneeling: A. Burton (Wakefield Trinity), J. Parkin (Wakefield Trinity), W. Batten (Hull -
Captain), A. A. Rosenfeld (Huddersfield), L. Land (Wakefield Trinity).*

Jimmy Kennedy

Hull/Rovers side beat a team of Australian soldiers 12-10, raising £83 for local charitable institutions. Steve Darmody tragically lost a foot while serving with the Motor Transport Section in Flanders and £220 was raised for him in a charity match. Billy Batten scored 18 tries and Jim Kennedy kicked 50 goals. Hull beat Halifax 69-2.

Seventy-seven players were used in 31 matches in 1916 when Hull Kingston Rovers and several West Riding Clubs generously provided players to enable Hull to fulfill fixtures. Lt. Jack Harrison was reported missing in action after the battle at Oppy Wood on 3rd May 1917 and he was to be awarded the Victoria Cross and the Military Cross posthumously for Valour. Regular "A"teamer Alf Taylor was also killed in action. Back home, Alf Francis scored 14 tries and Jim Kennedy kicked 54 goals.

The Northern Union flag was kept flying at the Boulevard in 1917 and Hull's record was 17 wins, and 7 defeats. With 261 points scored and 34 points against, they finished fourth in the League. A loss of £551 was made on the year, not helped by having to pay £164 Entertainment Tax. An appeal to endow a cot at Hull Royal Infirmary at Prospect Street to the memory of Lt. Jack Harrison, V.C., M.C., was launched and a flag day organised to help reach a target of £500.

Only six teams in Yorkshire were still playing in September 1918 but when the War finally came to an end, a new competition started in January 1919 with 11 teams and Hull topped the table with 13 wins out of 16 matches played, beating York 69-0 and Hunslet 62-7. Billy Batten received the Yorkshire League Cup from Mr. J.B. Cooke of Wakefield, President of the Northern Rugby Competition, at a smoking concert held in the Grosvenor Hotel in Carr Lane. Despite paying £1,074 in Entertainment Tax, a profit of £737 was made on the year. Club Secretary Alf Charlesworth resigned after fifteen years service and he was replaced by Charles Lofthouse. Top try scorer was Alf Francis with 35 and Billy Batten was runner-up with 27. Jimmy Kennedy kicked 79 goals.

Hull finished runners-up in the League in 1919 but they beat Fartowners 3-2 in the Championship play-off Final at Headingley. The average home gate was 11,515 and shareholders numbered 400. A profit of £2,667 was made on the year despite Entertainment Tax payments of £3,712. Over £15,000 was taken in gate receipts in the season, a club record. Nearly 19,000 paid £1,200 at the local derby match with Hull K.R. Billy Batten received £1,079 from his benefit. Four important signings were made:- Billy Stone, a pacey winger with a devastating side step and body swerve from Gloucester R.U; Eddie Caswell, a powerfully built player from Cardiff R.U; a mobile second-row forward, Bob Taylor from Barrow; and J.R. Cresswell. Stone had a meteoric start to his rugby league career and was selected to tour Australasia, scoring 24 tries, certainly a dream start for any rugby union convert. Local junior side, British Oil and Cake Mills (BOCM), were beaten 75-2 at the Boulevard in the first round of the Challenge Cup before a crowd of 12,000. Jim Kennedy totalled 181 points with 15 tries and 68 goals and Alf Francis crossed for 26 tries. Yorkshire county honours came to Billy Batten, Jack Holdsworth and Tommy Milner. Batley were beaten 60-3 in the League.

Mr. G.W. Miller was elected Chairman in 1920 and Jim Kennedy captained the side to a second successive championship play-off success when they beat Hull K.R. 16-14 in the Headingley Final. The "Robins" had finished at the top of the

1919/20

Back Row (l. to r.): J. Beasty, J. Devereux, T. Herridge, E. Caswell, F. Newsome, P. Oldham, J. Humphris.
Third Row: J. E. Wyburn, H. Garrett, R. Taylor, E. Shield, A. Grice, W. Holder, S. Melville (Trainer).
Sitting: A. J. Boynton (Chairman), J. Holdsworth, W. Batten J. E. Kennedy (Captain), T. Milner, S. Markham, C. N. Lofthouse (Secretary).
In Front: A. J. Francis, J. Hulme.

Billy Stone

G. W. Miller Esq.
Chairman 1920-1945

1920/21
Back Row (l. to r.): W. Batten (inset), J. Beasty, J. E. Wyburn, A. Grice, J. Ellis.
Third Row: F. Newsome, R. Taylor, W. Charles, E. Shield, T. Herridge, A. Francis,
J. Holdsworth.
Sitting: C. N. Lofthouse (Secretary), H. Garrett, E. Rogers, J. E. Kennedy (Captain),
J. Devereux, W. J. Stone, J. Humphris, G. W. Miller (Chairman).
In Front: T. Milner, E. Caswell.

40

League on percentage and had beaten Hull 2-0 in the Yorkshire Cup Final at Headingley. Over 24,000 paid £1,704 at the Christmas Day Derby with K.R. when the East Hull side won 15-6. Hull's average home gate during the season was 12,692. Local lad Jim Kennedy broke the club's points scoring record with 282 (114 goals and 18 tries) and he was presented with a gold watch to mark the achievement. He kicked 14 goals in the 79-2 victory over Rochdale Hornets and scored 36 points in the 80-7 win over Keighley. Billy Stone scored an impressive 40 tries in the season. The club totalled 781 points including big wins over Bradford Northern (60-4) and Wakefield Trinity (69-11). Representative honours came to Billy Batten (Captain of Yorkshire), G. Todd (Yorkshire), and Batten and Billy Stone played for England against Wales and against Other Nationalities. Deveraux, Herridge, Holder and Rogers received £350 each from their benefit. Billy Stone toured Australia.

Hull lost 10-21 to the Australian tourists in 1921 when Harold Horder, a winger with speed and swerve, was cheered from the field in what the Australian press called "a tribute from a highly partisan English crowd." Nearly £2,000 was spent on ground improvements. Edgar Morgan was signed on and was selected for England against Australia just 36 days after his debut for the club. Bowman and E. Gwynne also joined the Boulevarders together with G. Oliver, a Welsh R.U. International. Billy Batten and Billy Stone played in the same match as Morgan, and Bob Taylor played in the Third Test when the Ashes were regained. Third place in the League was attained although 8 matches had to be played in 18 days in a hectic finish to the season. Halifax, Hull K.R., Dewsbury and Wigan were knocked out of the Challenge Cup but Hull went down 9-10 to Rochdale Hornets in the Headingley Final. H. Garrett (24) and Bob Taylor (22) topped the club's try scoring list.

J.A. Dunkerley, J.P. was Hon. President in 1922, another of the club's most successful seasons. They finished top of the League with 30 wins out of 36 and had rare doubles over Wigan, St. Helens, Halifax and Hull K.R. They also reached the Final of the Challenge Cup for the second successive year, losing however 8-23 to Leeds at Wakefield after accounting for Broughton Rangers, Swinton, Salford and Wigan in earlier rounds. The Yorkshire League Cup was won and the 'A' team won the Yorkshire Senior Competition. Billy Stone was the club Captain and won an International Cap along with clubmates Billy Batten, Bob Taylor, Eddie Caswell, G. Oliver and Edgar Morgan. Stone scored 26 tries, Taylor 25 and Caswell 23, and Jim Kennedy kicked 81 goals. Fred Samuel, a Welsh R.U. International full back, was signed from Mountain Ash. A profit of £2,161 was made on the year.

The Great Depression of 1923 reduced gate receipts in Rugby League. For the first time in 16 attempts, the Yorkshire Cup was at last won when Huddersfield were beaten 10-4 at Headingley. *En route* to the Final they beat Bramley, Hunslet and Dewsbury. Billy Stone scored 27 tries and Jim Kennedy kicked 59 goals in a season when Head Groundsman T. Coates received £200 from a benefit match. Whitty and Bowman were selected for the Australian Tour and J.H. Dannatt went as Tour Manager.

Jim Kennedy succeeded D.E. Morgan as Captain in 1924 and after giving the club magnificent service, Billy Batten was transferred to Wakefield Trinity for

1923/24
Standing (l. to r.): J. Beasty, R. Taylor, H. Garrett, J. E. Kennedy, T. J. Collins,
C. E. Ellery, G. Oliver, H. Bowman.
Sitting: T. E. Gwynne, E. A. Caswell, E. Morgan (Captain), W. Batten, W. Brennan, R. Rogers.
In Front: S. Whitty, W. J. Stone.

£350. Hull K.R. objected to the League that their home games clashed with Hull City's home games more than Hull F.C.'s home games did, and a fairer fixture programme was drawn up and accepted. A feature of the season was the enormous amount of good the club did for charity - benefactors included the Spring Bank Orphanage, Hull Royal Infirmary, Hull and District Rugby Union (Accident Fund), Hull and East Riding Blind Institute, Dr. Barnardo's Home, Press Widows and Orphans Fund, National Institute for the Blind, St. Vincents Home, Newland Sailors Orphan Homes, Great War Trust, Hull Schools Rugby Union, and Hull and District Rugby Union Junior Playing Fields Society. And the club still made a profit of £289 on the season! Billy Stone scored 16 tries but after finishing 17th the previous season, the club slipped to 18th place and went out of the Challenge Cup and the Yorkshire Cup at the first hurdle.

The 1925 season was a great improvement on the previous two when fourth place was gained in the League and the club reached the semi-final of the Challenge Cup under the captaincy of Eddie Caswell. A first-ever victory was gained over Oldham at the Watersheddings. A crowd of 19,585 paid £1,307 at the home match against Warrington in the third round of the Challenge Cup and the average gate at the Boulevard was 6,212, while the "A" team averaged 2,005 at home and won the Yorkshire Senior Competition. The League matches against Hull K.R. were scheduled for Christmas Day and Good Friday for the next two seasons and gate money was to be pooled. Prolific scorer Billy Stone had to retire through injury and a benefit for this popular player brought him £437. The Boulevard under-16 junior side was formed and included Harold Ellerington, Ron Everitt and Harry Blinkhorn. Bob Taylor scored a remarkable 32 tries plus 4 in his three International games to achieve a club record for most tries in a season by a forward. A.E.Bateson kicked 50 goals.

Hull finished fifth in the League in 1926 and they won the Yorkshire League Cup. Castleford played at the Boulevard for the first time on 27th August. Bradford Northern were beaten 54-17. S. Errington and W.W. Thornton signed on. In an exciting match, Hull went down 13-15 to the All-Black tourists. During the season S. Pickering was an ever-present, T. Gwynne scored 22 tries and A.E. Bateson kicked 50 goals. H. Bowman and R. Taylor played for England against New Zealand. Greyhound racing was planned for the Boulevard during the summer months.

52 matches were played in 1927 when the semi-final of the Challenge Cup was reached and Dewsbury were the victors over the Boulevarders in the Yorkshire Cup Final held at Headingley. During the season the Club's President J.A. Dunkerley died. Wilson Hall, a New Zealand International, joined the club and Ron Everitt, H. Tasker and M. Short also signed on. E. Gwynne and H. Bowman were selected for the Australasia tour and the club's top scorers were W.J. Davies (14 tries) and A.E. Bateson (40 goals). The Secretary's salary was £400 per annum.

In 1928, Joe Oliver was signed on from Batley. He gave the Black and Whites great service over ten years and certainly deserved the title of the 'points machine'! The club Captain was H. Bowman. Top scorer was A.E. Bateson with 15 tries and Joe Oliver kicked 36 goals. A. Carmichael joined from east of the River Hull. The Boulevard Old Boys won the Under-20 League Cup while the Boulevard Juniors won their League Cup and the Hesslewood Orphanage Cup. A loss of £1,031 was made on the year but interest in the old club was tremendous.

The Australian tourists received a warm welcome from an appreciative Yorkshire crowd and trounced Hull 35-2. Gate receipts came to £959. M.G. Short's record run of 101 consecutive appearances ended and Bob Taylor was transferred to Barrow. All teams played an equal number of matches in the League and the percentage system of placings was stopped. A.E. Bateson kicked 39 goals and Joe Oliver crossed for 16 tries. Joe set a fine example as Captain in the 1929 season when he scored 155 points with 7 tries and 67 goals. The club finished 12th out of 28 in the League. Bickershaw Hornets were beaten 44-10 in the first round of the Challenge Cup. Hull slipped to 16th place in the League in 1930 but reached the semi-final of the Yorkshire Cup, losing to Leeds 4-9 at home. A loss of £60 was announced on the year. Keighley were beaten 52-15 in 1931 when Hull slipped again to 21st in the League. They reached the semi-final of the Yorkshire Cup again, this time losing to Hunslet 0-15 at home. G.W. Bateman continued his scoring record with 28 tries in his captaincy year. Joe Oliver totalled 146 points with 20 tries and 43 goals. C.R.Fifield came over from Australia and his partnership and understanding with Joe Oliver proved devastating for the Hull side. W. Teal also signed on. The Boulevard Juniors played such teams as Grapes, Day Street Recs., St. Mary's, Queens Hall, Cottingham, New Goodwin and Newton. Probably one of the finest full backs ever to wear the Number 1 jersey at the Boulevard signed in 1932. Freddie Miller joined the club from Crowle Street School. Bradford Northern were beaten 63-3 and Higginshaw were beaten 37-9 in the first round of the Challenge Cup.

Everitt T. Jackson was appointed Secretary in 1933 when a profit of £743 was

1927/28

Standing (l. to r.): A. Miller (Reserve), A. E. Bateson, H. Bowman, G. Oliver, R. Taylor, J. T. Smallwood, E. Wrigley (Trainer).

Sitting: A. Charlesworth (Secretary), E. Gwynne, S. Whitty, E. Caswell (Captain), W. Batten, E. Jenney, S. Pickering.

In Front: R. Garvey, Wilson Hall.

Joe Oliver

44

1932/33

Standing (l. to r.): Harold Bowman, Joe Oliver (Captain), J. W. Milner, Billy Stead,
George Bateman, Dick Fifield, Jack Dawson.
Front Row: Charlie Wilkinson, Billy Teal, Harold Ellerington, Ron Everitt,
Andrew Carmichael, Fred Winsor.

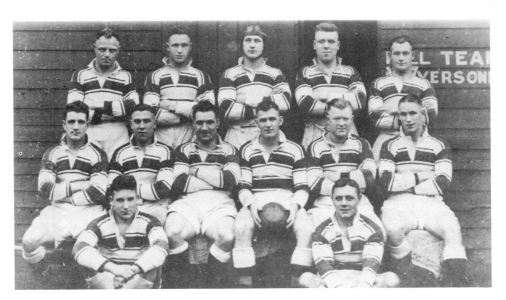

1934/35

Standing (l. to r.): Bateman, L. Barlow, Dawson, Stead, G. H. Barlow.
Sitting: Courtney, Miller, Carmichael, Oliver, Corner, Wilson.
Front Row: Herberts, Colling.

45

announced. The Christmas Day fixture with the Australian tourists brought receipts of £1,391, the highest sum for a club match on the tour. Hull lost 5-19 and they went down 23-26 to Jean Galia's French side. Joe Oliver kicked 98 goals and scored 19 tries totalling 253 points during the season. C. Wilkinson was an ever-present and Bob Corner and Fred Colling were signed from Hartlepool Rovers. G.W. Bateman was the club's leading try scorer with 21 and he also topped the list in 1934, touching down for 26 tries. Hull reached the semi-final of the Challenge Cup but lost 5-21 to Huddersfield at Headingley. It was around this time that the popularity of an American western song about a horse called 'Old Faithful' came into prominence and for whatever reason was adopted by the Hull supporters and has become the club's "Battle Hymn", heard on all rugby league grounds.

OLD FAITHFUL

Old Faithful, we rode the range together,
Old Faithful, in every kind of weather
When your round up days are over,
There'll be pastures white with clover,
For you, Old Faithful, pal of mine.

Hurry up Old fella,
Cos the moon is yeller tonight,
Hurry up Old fella,
Cos the moon is mellow and bright.
There's a coyote howling to the moon above,
So carry me back to the one I love,
Hurry up Old fella, cos we gotta get home tonight.

Old Faithful, we rode the range together,
Old Faithful, in every kind of weather,
When your round up days are over,
There'll be pastures white with clover,
For you, Old Faithful, pal of mine.

Yippy yip yip, old hoss,
There's food and rest
An you've done your best old hoss,
Oh, carry me over the mountain ridge,
Down that trail to the old pine bridge,
To my gal Lily,
Bunkhouse Billy and the boss.

Old Faithful, we rode the range together,
Old Faithful, in every kind of weather,
When your round up days are over,
There'll be pastures white with clover,
For you, Old Faithful, pal of mine.

1935/36

Standing (l. to r.): E. Caswell (Trainer), C. Booth, L. Thacker, G. Barlow, S. Wilson,
W. Stead, R. Corner, G. W. Bateman, L. Barlow.
Sitting: E. Overton, C. R. Fifield, Mr. G. W. Miller (Chairman), J. Oliver (Captain),
Mr. J. H. Dannatt (Vice-Chairman), F. Miller, A. Carmichael.
In Front: E. Herbert, W. J. Courtney.
Absent: H. Ellerington (Australian Tour 1936), J. R. P. Dawson (Unable to attend),
C. G. Gouldstone (injured).

Joe Oliver had another successful season scoring 21 tries and kicking 83 goals, totalling 229 points. The club's other leading try scorers were C. Fifield (16) and E. Herbert and J. Corner (both with 15). Hull beat Jean Galia's touring side from France once again, this time 24-20. A profit of £1,722 on the season included a donation of £60 from the Supporters Club. Local talent on Hull's playing fields was closely watched and Albert Bowers and Charlie Booth signed on the dotted line in 1935. Great success was gained on the field, the League Championship was won, with Liverpool City runners-up. Widnes were whacked 21-2 in the play-off at Headingley. Over 700 points were scored in all matches and once again Joe Oliver contributed most with 85 goals and 27 tries, followed by C. Gouldstone and E. Herbert both of whom scored 19 tries. Freddie Miller was an ever-present. A profit of £2,462 was made on the season and the greyhound racing equipment was sold for £850. C. Thacker, J. Dawson, C. Booth and H. Ellerington gained international honours and Ellerington toured Australia. He was Captain in 1936 when Frank Hurley joined the club from 'Down Under' and Freddie Miller equalled Short's record of playing in 101 consecutive matches for the club. This record still stands as does the ground capacity record set up that year when Hull entertained

1938/39

Back Row (l. to r.): E. Herbert, W. Morrell, S. Wilson, R. Corner, L. Thacker, L. Barlow, C. Booth.
In front: S. Brogden, F. Miller, H. Ellerington (Captain), E. Overton, J. A. Johnson, G. Barlow.

Leeds in the third round of the Challenge Cup, watched by a crowd of 28,798. Hull lost 4-5 and had Joe Oliver and George Barlow sent off. Earlier on in the season these two players had been instrumental in setting up a fine 13-12 win over Wigan, gained with a late try which sent the crowd into raptures and Gene Autry's rendering of 'Old Faithful' was taken up all round the Boulevard. A match against Hunslet for the Hull Great War Trust raised £98. "Mr. Points Scorer", Joe Oliver, totalled 196 with 16 tries and 74 goals while C.R. Fifield touched down for 18 tries, and J. Corner and S. Wilson scored 17 apiece. Bramley were beaten 61-7.

Three great servants of the club over many years died in 1937, J.H. Dannatt, F.C. Foster and C.E. Rymer. Ernie Lawrence, a product of Blenkin Street School and St. Mary's, signed on. Joe Oliver kicked 60 goals and the club finished 13th out of 29. A profit of £1,158 was announced.

Harold Ellerington was club Captain in 1938 and the club reached the Yorkshire Cup Final but went down 10-18 to Huddersfield at Odsal. Stanley Brogden was signed from Leeds for a fee of £1,200 and Freddie Miller kicked 101 goals. The club's 'A' team won their championship shield. A loss of £852 was announced.

THE END OF AN ERA

Only three League matches and one Yorkshire cup tie were played at the start of the 1939 season before the government banned football after the outbreak of the Second World War. A regional competition commenced with fifteen clubs agreeing to take part and Hull finished third. Jack Tindall had signed on for the club.

The A.G.M. in 1940 was held in the Imperial Hotel, Paragon Street, a place which teams, referees, players, officials and supporters had used over many years. Members heard of a loss of £683. Serious damage was caused to the ground by enemy bombing. The Boulevard/Hessle Road district was close to the city's docks and in a prime target area. Thirty-three of the club's registered players were serving in his Majesty's Forces but despite this, Hull was the only club to rely solely on registered players and finished runners-up to Bradford Northern in the Yorkshire Section. In the Challenge Cup, which had been suspended in the previous year, Hull went out to Batley and lost to York in the Yorkshire Cup.

The club had to rely on 'outside' players in 1941 when Ramsden, Clarke and the Beaumont Brothers from Hull K.R. together with Glynn from Huddersfield helped Hull to fulfill fixtures. Only 18 League matches were played, twelve were won and six lost but because of cup ties and severe weather plus some difficulties in raising a team, Hull didn't play a match between 3rd January and 28th March. They finished fourth out of 17 teams in the 'War League'.

1940/41

Standing (l. to r.): R. Corner, G. A. Pinder, R. Taylor, H. Bedford, G. W. Beales, W. Dockar, A. E. Allen, L. Thacker, E. Caswell (Trainer).
Sitting: E. Herbert, H. Mills, P. Ingram, S. Brogden (Captain), S. Hattersley, M. Daddy, R. Monkhouse.

A loss of £975 was made on the year and £720 was spent on 'emergency' re-building and ground maintenance.

Huddersfield, Swinton and Hull K.R. loaned some of their players in 1942 and helped to keep the club going. Sales of passes were only £36 and a loss of £406 was announced on the season. Hull finished 11th out of fourteen teams in the War League (St. Helens were bottom!). Ernie Herbert died a few days after his discharge from the Army and Jack Dawson died on duty with the RAF.

Players from Wakefield Trinity, Hull K.R., Swinton and Huddersfield were granted permission to play for Hull in 1943 if they were serving with the Armed Forces or were working in essential occupations in the area. Laurie Barlow earned the Military Medal for campaign conduct with the Forces in the Middle East, keeping up the club's great traditions. Hull finished third out of sixteen in the War Time League and lost 10-27 to Wigan in the play-offs. Huddersfield knocked the club out of the Challenge Cup and for the second successive year out of the Yorkshire Cup, all on a 'two leg' basis. A loss of just £29 was announced.

Eight matches out of 23 were won in the 1944 War League, when Hull K.R., Castleford, Salford, Swinton and Huddersfield kindly loaned players. A fine sporting spirit existed at the Boulevard although early demob of players was looked forward to. A loss of £14 was made on the season. Hull had kept their proud record of playing continuously throughout their long history.

THE IMMEDIATE POST-WAR PERIOD

The sporting scene tried hard to get back on its feet after the war had ended. Playing gear in the club's official colours was hard to come by but supporters rallied round. Enough clothing coupons were gathered and Kenningtons offered a laundry service. A.G. Middleton was club Secretary and C. Booth captained the side in 1945. G.W. Miller died after twenty-six years as Chairman and he was succeeded by F.P. Collins. A remarkable number of players was used, 46 in all and new signings included Watts, Glynn and Sinclair while Brogden was transferred to Rochdale. Transfer fees brought in £1400, a profit of £139 was made on sale of programmes and a working profit of £3312 was made on the season, although £4614 had to be paid out in Entertainment Tax.

The popular full-back Freddie Miller was appointed Captain in 1946 when Secretary L. Pattison announced a profit of £1737 at the club's A.G.M. held in the Hull Church Institute in Albion Street. £1387 was spent on ground re-building and £491 realised through the sales of passes. A club house at 193 Boulevard was valued at £1263. After beating Featherstone Rovers over two legs and then York and Hull K.R., Hull lost 0-10 to Wakefield Trinity in the Yorkshire Cup Final at Headingley. Freddie Miller kicked 106 goals and Ernie Lawrence scored 21 tries during the season. The club's first all-ticket match was against Hull K.R. at the Boulevard.

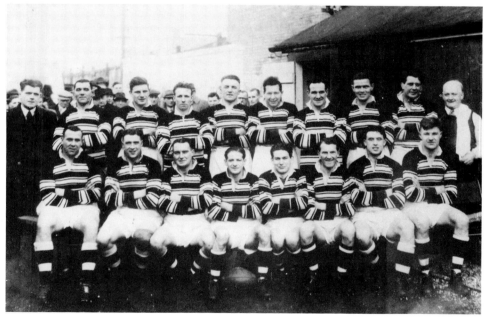

1947/48
Standing (l. to r.): E. Tattersfield (Coach), C. Booth, H. Evans, R. Jewitt, J. Tindall, B. Ryan, J. Sullivan, R. Kavanagh, G. Watt, E. Caswell (Trainer).
Sitting: F. Miller, E. Bedford, B. Madden, E. Lawrence (Captain), D. Jackson, A. Bowers, A. Bedford, A. Sinclair.

G. Eric Miller was elected Chairman in 1947 and Ernie Hardaker became Vice-chairman. Former Secretary E.T. Jackson died. The first post-war tourists were New Zealand and they were given a warm welcome to the Boulevard but lost 7-13. Ernie Lawrence was club Captain and Charlie Booth and Freddie Miller were granted a joint benefit match against Oldham. Miller celebrated by kicking 89 goals in the season.

A trio of Australians joined the club and quickly became favourites of the "Threepenny Standers". Bruce Ryan, George Watt and Duncan Jackson blended into the side and other signings were B. Madden (from Huddersfield), Hagan Evans (Bradford) and E. Bedford (Hull K.R.). Ryan led the try scorers list with 24, J. Sullivan scored 18 and Albert Bower touched down for 16 and also played in two internationals. The sale of passes realised £761 and a profit of £749 was announced on the year. The 'A' team beat Castleford 8-2 in the Yorkshire Senior Competition before a record crowd of 9,000.

George Watt was Captain in 1948 and the Aussie welcomed his compatriots Keith Gittoes and John Payne, bringing Hull's quota of Australians to five. Other newcomers to the Boulevard senior club were Mick Scott (Boulevard Juniors), Carl Turner (Kenfighill), B. Conway (Fitzwilliam), Tom Danter (Brigend), W.G. Jones (Cardiff) plus H. Boagey and Les Baxter. The 'A' team won their League and Challenge Cup. Attendances were booming in a sport starved area and £1503 worth of passes were sold, while £737 was spent on ground improvements. Harold Ellerington was granted a benefit by the Board of Directors. Hagan Evans played for Wales against France and T. Hart kicked 48 goals during the season. Bruce Ryan went over for 12 tries and 19 matches out of 36 were won.

Former player and coach Eddie Caswell tragically died at the Boulevard on 22nd May.

TEAM RE-BUILDING COMMENCES AND SUCCESS IS SWEET

The 1949 season was the beginning of what was to be a very successful period for the West Hull side. A master stroke was the signing of Roy Francis from Warrington and he was later to prove a competent coach. D. Burnell was signed from Batley and Tommy Harris and Bill Hopkins were Welsh R.U. converts from Newbridge. Hull officials wanted to give trials to Harris because they thought he was too small for a hooker. Bill Hopkins told them "Well I can pack down with him and Welsh R.U. forwards are as big as Rugby League props". Four favourites left the Boulevard - Freddie Miller moved to Featherstone Rovers, Bruce Ryan was transferred to Leeds for £4750, Joe Sullivan signed for York and A. Sinclair joined Hunslet. The French club, Marseilles, was entertained. In the annual report, tributes were paid to former players Jack Townend and ex-Secretary Alf Charlesworth, who had died during the season. Mr. Hardaker was once again congratulated on his programme notes. A loss of £917 was announced. The 'A' team completed a League and Cup double for the second year in succession. T.W. Hart kicked 65 goals and Bruce Ryan scored 25 tries before his move to Leeds.

Ernie Hardaker was elected Chairman in 1950 and Roy Francis was club Captain. Team building began in earnest with new faces at the club including Colin Hutton (signed from Widnes), Johnny Whiteley (Hull Boys Club), Jim Drake (Heworth), Des Foreman (Wakefield Trinity) and C. Knapp (Fenners). Bernard Poole was transferred to Leeds and Hagan Evans and T. Danter moved to Dewsbury. T.W. Hart kicked 66 goals and skipper Francis touched down 12 times. A club house at 22 Parkfield Drive was valued at £1711.

Roy was appointed full-time coach in 1951 and the result was that Hull finished third in the League with doubles over Leeds, St. Helens, Barrow, Featherstone, Hull K.R., Bramley, Castleford, Keighley and Cardiff. Team building continued with Harry Markham, Bill Drake and Bob Coverdale joining the club. George Watt moved to Rochdale and W.G. Ward from Wigan was appointed Secretary. A civic welcome was given to the New Zealand tourists at Hull Guildhall after Hull had lost 8-28 to the Kiwis. Mick Scott became an England international and Tommy Harris was selected for Wales, while top points scorers were Ivor Watts (19 tries), Keith Gittoes (17 tries), and T. Hart kicked 74 goals and scored 6 tries to total 166 points. Ernie Lawrence was granted a benefit. A club house at 11 Boulevard was valued at £1660 and a profit of £1637 was made on the year. Two Division rugby was turned down by the majority of member clubs.

Hull were very unlucky with injuries during the 1952 season and the new play-the-ball rule was not an immediate success. The Australians beat the club 28-0 and were entertained at the Hull Guildhall and toured the premises of Reckitt and Colman. Colin Hutton captained the side on many occasions and new additions to the playing staff were J. Watkinson, A. Tripp, N. Hockley and A. Moat while Keith Gittoes returned to Australia. Mick Scott and Johnny Whiteley played for Yorkshire and England, Tommy Harris for Wales, and Harry Markham for Yorkshire, while T.W. Hart kicked 41 goals and scored 3 tries. Top try scorer was Ivor Watts with 19. Over £3000 had to be paid in Entertainment Tax.

High quality rugby was played in the 1953 season. Colin Hutton broke the club's points scoring record with 303, made up of 144 goals and 4 tries, and he was

Tommy Harris

*Power and determination
from Johnny Whiteley*

1951/52

Standing (l. to r.): Tom Harris, Arthur Bedford, Tom Hart, Robin Coverdale, Harry Markham, John Whiteley, Colin Hutton, Jim Drake.
Front: Mick Scott, Bernard Conway, Roy Francis (Captain), Don Burnell, Ivor Watts.

1954/55

(l. to r.): John Whiteley, Mick Scott, Arthur Bedford, Norman Hackley, Colin Hutton, Bernard Conway, Albert Tripp, Roy Francis (Captain-Coach), Tom Harris, Ivor Watts, Carl Turner, Robin Coverdale, Bill Riches, Bill Drake, Harry Markham.

1955/56

Standing (l. to r.): Robin Coverdale, John Whiteley, Bill Drake, Bill Riches, Jim Drake, Brian Cooper, Keith Bowman, G. W. Sharpley (Masseur).
Seated: John Watkinson, Ivor Watts, Roy Francis (Coach), Mick Scott (Captain), Carl Turner, Colin Hutton, Tom Harris.
Front: Finn, Bernard Conway, Rowley Moat.

presented with a barometer to mark the occasion. Keith Bowman was signed from Hunslet and he was an ever-present, playing 46 matches. He also topped the try scorers list with 33, followed by Ivor Watts who went over for 32. Bill Riches came to the club from Batley and George Langfield from St. Helens. The away local derby against Hull K.R. was played under floodlights at Boothferry Park, home of Hull City A.F.C., Hull winning 15-4. After beating Bramley over two legs, Halifax and Hunslet, the Black and Whites lost 2-7 to Bradford Northern in the Yorkshire Cup Final at Headingley. Representative honours came to the club's players again - Tommy Harris toured Australia and England caps came to Johnny Whiteley, Mick Scott and Harry Markham, and they also played for Yorkshire together with Keith Bowman and under the captaincy of Bill Riches. Ivor Watts turned out for Cumberland. Extensive ground improvements were carried out. The two-legged system of matches in both the Yorkshire Cup and the Challenge Cup was due to be abolished in the following season.

Inconsistency was the reason for the drop to 19th place in the League in 1954. Doncaster were beaten 61-7, Dewsbury 55-5, Batley 39-2, and Workington 31-4 but Warrington, Leeds, Hunslet and Bramley completed the double over the Airlie Birds. They reached the Yorkshire Cup Final for the second successive season but lost again, this time 14-22 to Halifax at Headingley. Club Secretary W.G. Ward resigned. The supporters section opened a new clubhouse on the ground and the club's directors appealed for more support on the terraces. Alan Holdstock and Geoff Cole were signed on from local rugby, and Stan Cowan (Scottish R.U.) and Tommy Finn (St. Helens) joined Hull. Colin Hutton scored 223 points with 110 goals and a single try and Keith Bowman touched down 22 tries. Johnny Whiteley and Bob Coverdale were members of the victorious Great Britain World Cup Squad.

First class entertainment was provided on the rugby field in the 1955 season. The club reached the Yorkshire Cup Final for the third successive season but completed a hat trick of defeats when after a 10-10 draw against Halifax at Headingley, they went down 0-7 in the replay at Odsal. Revenge was sweet when they met Halifax in the Championship Final at Maine Road, Manchester, home of Manchester City A.F.C. Hull had finished fourth in the League and beat Warrington 17-0 in the semi-final. A crowd of 37,000 at Maine Road saw a hard tussle. Harris and Finn scored tries for Hull and Hutton kicked a single goal, but Halifax were 9-8 in the lead until a dramatic last minute penalty goal was superbly planted over the bar by Colin Hutton from right out on the touchline. During a great personal season, Colin kicked 144 goals and scored 2 tries to total 294 points. Roly Moat scored 31 tries and representative honours came to Harry Markham, Mick Scott, Johnny Whiteley, Bill Riches and Keith Bowman, all selected for Yorkshire. Bill Drake and Ivor Watts turned out for Cumberland, and Tommy Harris for Wales. Arthur Bedford and Ivor Watts shared a benefit. R. Cassels was appointed Secretary. The New Zealand tourists beat the host club 17-12. Blackpool were beaten 56-13. Electric lights were fixed to the Boulevard's East Stand which meant training could now be carried out at the ground instead of indoors at Madeley Street. A clubhouse at 22 Parkfield Drive was sold at a profit of just £7.

An excellent team spirit ran through the whole club in 1956 and this was reflected on the field of play when second place in the League was gained and 930 points scored. An innovation was the "European Club Championship" when Hull and Halifax were invited to compete with French clubs Carcassonne and Albi. The League matches against Halifax counted and Hull won 35-12 and 14-10, beat Carcassonne twice and had a win and a draw against Albi, giving Hull the championship. As this was the only time it was competed for, then Hull are still officially European Champions of the Rugby League World. After hammering Barrow 45-14 in the semi-final of the play-offs at Boothferry Park, Hull went down to Oldham 14-15 at Odsal. Indirectly, Hull's defeat led to a change of rule as Cyril Sykes was penalised for not playing the ball because he was injured and Oldham kicked the resultant penalty. The rule was amended so that recovery time was given to the injured player and play re-started when he was fit. $1^{1}/_{4}$ miles of new drains were laid under the pitch and maintenance costs came to £4,527 in the season but despite this and £6,078 paid in Entertainment Tax, the club still made a profit of £4,800. Over £2,000 of that came from the sale of season passes. A joint Hull and Rovers thirteen lost 14-37 to the powerful Australian tourists at Boothferry Park. During the season Ivor Watts scored 29 tries and Colin Hutton broke his own club record by kicking 166 goals and 1 try, registering 335 points.

The ever-popular Johnny Whiteley, "Gentleman John" as he was known, was

1956 R.L. CHAMPIONSHIP CUP WINNERS.
Back Row (l. to r.): C. Hutton, R. Coverdale, J. Whiteley, W. Drake, H. Markham,
B. Cooper, J. Watkinson, K. Bowman.
Front Row: B. Darlington, C. Turner, M. Scott (Captain), T. Finn, T. Harris.

elected Captain in 1957 and in another excellent season, Hull finished fourth in the League with big victories over Dewsbury (62-5), Doncaster (56-2), Castleford (45-2 and 52-2), Bramley (58-2), Wigan (37-5), Huddersfield (43-8) and Barrow (59-5), totalling 987 points during the season. For the third successive season, Hull reached the finals of the play-off and they beat Workington Town by the comprehensive margin of 20-3 at Odsal. Top try scorers were Ivor Watts (29) and Tommy Finn (23) while Peter Bateson kicked 131 goals. New signings included Frank Broadhurst, Brian Hambling and Eddie Wanklyn. Tommy Harris, Johnny Whiteley and Jim Drake were selected for the Australian tour but Drake had to withdraw because of injury. Harris and Whiteley also played in the Great Britain World Cup team. The 'A' team won the Yorkshire Senior Competition Challenge Cup. On the financial side, travelling costs for the season came to £1,264. Entertainment Tax was £1,048 and the Supporters Club donated £1,300 from their pools operation.

RUGBY LEAGUE CHAMPIONS - 1957/58

Standing (l. to r.): A. Holdstock (inset), P. Whiteley, S. Cowan, M. Scott, B. Saville,
G. Sharpley (Trainer), G. Dannatt (inset).
Sitting: B. Cooper, C. Cole, C. Sykes, B. Hambling, R. Francis (Coach), J. Whiteley (Captain),
T. Harris, J. Drake, W. Drake.
Front Row: C. Turner, P. Bateson, I. Watts, F. Broadhurst, T. Finn, G. Harrison.

Arthur Keegan

Wembley was reached for the first time in 1958. In the earlier rounds, Hull beat Blackpool Borough, Wakefield Trinity, Hull Kingston Rovers and Featherstone Rovers to qualify to meet Wigan in the final. However, the team did not do itself justice and Wigan played some grand rugby to win 30-13. The Yorkshire Cup final was reached but defeat loomed again and they went down 14-15 to Featherstone Rovers at Headingley. 928 points were scored in the season with main contributions from G. Matthews (23 tries) and Peter Bateson (99 goals). Arthur Keegan, Dick Boustead and Tom Sutton had joined the Boulevarders and Mick Scott and R. Turner shared a benefit. A. Smith was appointed Secretary. Big wins were notched against Keighley (58-15) and Doncaster (53-8).

The famous twin-towers of Wembley welcomed Hull once again in 1959. That season York, Keighley, Wigan and Oldham were overcome and Wakefield Trinity were the opposition, but in a final graced by the presence of Her Majesty Queen Elizabeth, Hull's injury problems before and during the final proved their downfall and they lost heavily 5-38. At least they had the consolation of Tommy Harris being awarded the Lance Todd Trophy. Mike Smith made history by being the first player to make his first team debut at Wembley. Earlier in the season Sam Evans and Nan Halafihi had joined the club and Tommy Harris and Brian Cooper were awarded a joint 10 year benefit. Ivor Watts was appointed assistant coach. The Drake twins, Jim and Bill, played for Cumberland and top scorers were

Wembley 1959
Hull players and officials inspect the "hallowed turf".

Tommy Finn (23 tries) and Peter Bateson, registering 328 points with 161 goals and 2 tries. He was very unlucky to be injured just before the Challenge Cup Final and so missed out on a Wembley appearance. A combined Hull and Rovers side lost 9-29 to Australia at Boothferry Park. Travelling expenses amounted to £2154 in the season.

It was a common complaint among Hull fans at this time that the club had the forwards but lacked the backs. However another successful cup run in 1960 seemed to refute this. A third successive final was on the cards but St. Helens were too strong and Hull went down 9-26 in the semi-final at Odsal. The club was going through a transitional period. Johnny Whiteley and Jim Drake shared a 10 year benefit and Whiteley and Tommy Harris were selected for the World Cup Series. Newcomers to the Boulevard were: David Doyle-Davidson, Dick Gemmell, Charles Booth and Keith Barnwell. Ron Tate was appointed groundsman. Nearly £3,000 was taken from the sale of season passes. Peter Bateson kicked 85 goals and Terry Hollindrake touched down for 18 tries.

INCONSISTENT YEARS

For the first time in thirty years, Hull finished below Hull K.R. in the 1961 season but a combined Hull/Rovers XIII beat the New Zealand tourists 17-6 at the Boulevard. A loss of £3,902 was announced despite nearly £8,000 received from transfer fees which included Jim Drake moving across the city to Craven Park. Tommy Harris moved to York as coach to the Minstermen. Bill Drake was granted a benefit, and destined to become one of Hull's most popular players was Clive Sullivan who signed on together with John Edson, Jim Macklin and Wilf Rosenberg. Top of the try scorers list for the second successive season was Terry Hollindrake with 21 and Peter Bateson kicked 66 goals.

It was back to two divisions in 1962 and an Eastern championship preceded the League proper. Johnny Whiteley had to miss the whole of the season through an injury received in a pre-season charity match. Relegation was just avoided. New signings were Roger Booth and Norman Hockley, and Wilf Rosenberg (17 tries) and Arthur Keegan (81 goals) topped the scorers list.

During the summer of 1962, Hull and Rovers made a rugby league promotional tour of south-west England, playing each other three times, at Penzance, Cambourne and Falmouth, and Hull won all three matches. Match fees, expenses and win bonuses were on offer. Over 5,000 watched one of the matches when the local corporation who owned the field had to find another set of goalposts because their Rugby Union tenant club refused to let theirs be used. David Doyle-Davidson told me of one incident in the first match when after ten minutes of the game someone from the crowd yelled "when are you lot going to start fighting?" So much for rugby league's image! On the tour Arthur Keegan mis-fielded a high kick and was mortified to hear a shout from the stand "bring back Peter Bateson". Arthur ruefully observed "all this way and there's still someone from the threepenny stand here."

Hull were relegated in 1963 when they finished bottom of Division One with just four wins, against Keighley (two), Wakefield Trinity and Widnes. Roy Francis left the club for Leeds after guiding them through some of their most successful years and Johnny Whiteley was appointed club coach. New faces at the club were Jim Neale, Alan McGlone, Ken Huxley, Joe Brown, Chris Davidson, and Eric Brown, plus a new groundsman, Fred Daddy. Arthur Keegan kicked 47 goals and played two games for Yorkshire. Terry Devonshire was the top try scorer with 12. To complete a disastrous season, the club made a loss of £2,063. Terry Hollindrake and Bill Drake were transferred.

The 100th annual report of the Hull Football Club in 1964 announced a return to one division rugby and a respectable position of 13th out of 30 clubs was attained. In the new top 16 play-offs, Hull lost 9-15 to Wakefield Trinity in the first round. Ken Foulkes, Mike Harrison, Shaun O'Brien and Nick Trotter were signed and the season's leading scorers were Clive Sullivan with 18 tries and Eric Broom who kicked 75 goals. The club's former honorary doctor, Dr. Ian G. Innes, died. A profit of £169 was reported on the sale of the club centenary brochure compiled by Reg Lee and Albert Saville. David Doyle-Davidson was the first 'substitute' to be used when he replaced Terry Devonshire on 5th September against Batley in the first round of the Yorkshire Cup.

1961

Back Row (l. to r.): B. Hambling, J. Drake, C. Sykes, W. Drake, M. Scott, P. Bateson.
Middle Row: G. Harrison, G. Matthews, J. Whiteley, T. Harris, T. Hollindrake.
Front Row: J. Kershaw, T. Finn, F. Broadhurst, B. Saville.

Former club Captain Joe Oliver died during the 1965 season when Arthur Keegan was current Captain. John Maloney had joined the club from Shaw Cross, Dewsbury, and kicked 84 goals and scored 7 tries in his first season. He is currently the club record goal kicker with 674 in his career. Speedy winger Clive Sullivan touched down for 23 tries. An interesting item to compare with recent balance sheets is that players wages amounted to £8,147. The 'A' team won the Yorkshire Senior Challenge Cup. The first team's playing record was twenty wins, fourteen defeats and they scored 447 points while conceding 346.

Hull finished ninth in the League in 1966 but they were an "up and down side". Clive Sullivan finished at the top of the try scorers list again with 28 and John

E. Hardaker Esq.
Chairman 1964

1965
New Zealand centre Leo Brown brings down Arthur Keegan.

1965/66
Back Row (l. to r.): Brown (sub), Whiteley (Coach), McGlone, Broom, J. Macklin,
C. Sullivan, Harrison, Johnson, Neale, C. Booth (sub).
Front: Stocks, Devonshire, Keegan, Carmichael, Huxley, Foulkes.

John Maloney

65

1967

Back Row (l. to r.): John Stimpson (Masseur), G. Stocks, N. Oliver, M. Harrison,
J. Macklin, E. Broom, N. Trotter, J. Edson, A. McGlone, J. Whiteley (Coach).
Front Row: C. Davidson. K. Barnwell, D. Doyle-Davidson, T. Devonshire, A. Keegan,
T. Maloney, M. Lunn, B. Hancock.

1966

Back Row (l. to r.): A. McGlone, G. Pearson, C. Booth, R. Booth, C. Sykes, J. Macklin,
N. Oliver, G. Stocks.
Front Row: K. Foulkes, J. Maloney, A. Keegan, T. Devonshire, D. Doyle-Davidson.

April 1969
*The Boulevard pitch is ploughed up, the first stage of a plan to restore it to its former glory.
The stand is known throughout the rugby league world as the "Threepenny Stand", so called
because of the threepence transfer which had to be paid to use the stand.*

Maloney totalled 267 points. Club Director P. Bradley retired. A loss of £4,746 was sustained on the year. Arthur Keegan toured Australia.

Mr. J.L. Spooner was elected Club Chairman in 1967 but resigned in the following January. Cyril Fowler was appointed Club Secretary. Ken Owens, an Aussie hooker, made his debut and Clive Sullivan was selected for the World Cup Series squad and during the season crossed for seven tries in a 57-6 away win over Doncaster, still a club individual try scoring record. Floodlights were installed at the Boulevard at a cost of £7,138 and Hull lost 8-12 to Rovers in a preliminary TV floodlight trophy match. Hull beat Castleford, Halifax and Leeds to reach the Yorkshire Cup Final when in a hard fought match they went down to local rivals Hull K.R. 7-8 at Headingley. Chris Davidson was awarded the White Rose "man of the match" trophy. During the season, former club captain and international Mick Scott died.

Reg Lee was the Chairman of the club in 1968 and he saw new signings Len

Casey, Howard Firth from local Rugby Union, Don Robson and Keith Boxall, but despite this first round defeats were suffered in the Yorkshire Cup, the Challenge Cup and the Championship play-off. A net profit of £1,530 was a welcome sign and this included £250 for the franchise for selling hot dogs on match days. Arthur Keegan played for Great Britain against France.

Charles Watson took over as Club Chairman in February of the 1969/70 season. Earlier in the season the Yorkshire Cup was won for only the second time in the history of the club when Featherstone Rovers were beaten 12-9 in the final at Headingley. Joe Brown won the White Rose " man of the match" trophy. Johnny Whiteley was appointed Assistant Manager on the Australia/New Zealand tour and Clive Sullivan was selected on the playing side. Arthur Keegan had a benefit year and played for Great Britain against France. Players to move on from the Boulevard were Jim Neale, John Edson and Jim Macklin while Terry Kirchin, a ball-distributing forward, joined the club.

October 1968
Another touchline run ends in Clive Sullivan scoring a first half try against Huddersfield.

*Club Chairman
Charles Watson*

Ivor Watts was appointed club coach in 1970 and eighth position in the League was reached. A profit of £4,861 was announced and this figure included £510 from a speedway franchise and £300 from a catering franchise. David Doyle-Davidson was granted a benefit and Mick Crane joined the club from local junior club, Embassy. Clive Sullivan had a good season in 1971 when the Boulevarders finished a disappointing 19th out of 30. In the newly-introduced John Player Trophy, Hull beat Dewsbury, after a draw, and Keighley before going out to St. Helens at Knowsley Road. Local lad Keith Tindall followed his father by signing on and Mick Kendle, Steve Portz and Ron Cowan were also signed. Moves were made by John Maloney (to York), Arthur Keegan (to Bramley) and Chris Forster (to Huddersfield). The speedway franchise (£3,213) and TV income (£3,673) helped the club to announce a profit of £3,699 and the club's freehold property was valued at £30,000. Tragically former Chairman Ernie Hardaker died after a road accident and the deaths also occurred of former directors Frank Giblin and Reg Lee during the season.

The club Chairman in 1972 was Mr. C. Clegg when playing results were disastrous. The club finished 25th out of 30 clubs and they were relegated to the re-introduced Second Division in the following season. Wakefield Trinity thrashed the Black and Whites 52-0. Forty eight players were used during the season so obviously it was never possible to field a settled side. Malcolm Walker, Alan

1970

Back Row (l. to r.): H. Firth, K. Boxall, A. Macklin, T. Kirchin, M. Harrison, P. Ibbertson, C. Forster.
Front Row: B. Hancock, M. Owbridge, C. Sullivan, C. Davidson, K. Huxley, A. McGlone.

1972

Back Row (l. to r.): K. Boxall, M. Crane, N. Trotter, M. Harrison, H. Aston, M. Kendle, R. Firth, S. Portz.
Front Row: K. Foulkes, A. Macklin, C. Sullivan, T. Devonshire, B. Hancock.

Wardell, Brian Waltham and Tony Salmon joined the club. Attendances dropped and so sparse were some crowds that players could spot the fan yelling abuse at them! At least player/coach Clive Sullivan brought honour to the club when he captained Great Britain in their World Cup victory and appeared as the main subject of the 'This is your Life' television programme. It was no surprise when a loss of £9,500 was reported on the season.

Former player David Doyle-Davidson was appointed club coach in 1973 when member clubs voted to play on a Sunday in preference to a Saturday. Clive Sullivan left the Boulevard to join Hull K.R. and Mick Harrison, rated as the best No.8 to play for the club, joined Leeds for £10,000. Sixth position out of fourteen was reached in the League and although a profit of £802 was made, season passes brought in only £843 and programme sales suffered a loss of £24.

Two important signings were made in 1974. The experienced forward Bill Ramsey signed from Bradford Northern and George Clark came to Hull from New Hunslet. Despite these two signings, Hull could only finish 8th out of 14 in the second division. They did reach the semi-final of the Yorkshire Cup, losing 6-8 at home to Wakefield Trinity, but they suffered early exits from the Challenge Cup, the John Player Trophy and the BBC TV Floodlit Trophy.

SUCCESS IS JUST AROUND THE CORNER

Hull had a great run in the 1975 John Player Trophy when they beat Doncaster, Leeds, St. Helens and Salford on the way to a final against Widnes at Headingley. The 'Chemics' went into an 8-0 lead, but Hull levelled it at half-time and a real upset looked likely but pace and forward power told in the end and Widnes won 19-13. However, Hull made many friends with their gutsy display. In the League, Leigh gained fourth place on points difference to win promotion to the First Division at the expense of Hull.

Charles Watson was Club Chairman and Peter Darley was Secretary in 1976 when, under the captaincy of Brian Hancock, they finished top of the Second Division, winning twenty-two matches out of twenty-six. The average home gate was 3,860. Newcomers to the club were Keith Hepworth, David Marshall, Graham Bray and Mick Sutton while Bill Ramsey was transferred to Widnes. Tony Banham moved to Doncaster, Len Casey to Hull K.R., and Barry Kear to Oldham. Nick Trotter was awarded a benefit. Season passes brought in £1,720, the programme and souvenir shop made a profit of £329 and the speedway franchise brought in £6,138. Former players Billy Stone and Jimmy Kennedy died during the season.

The average home gate in 1977 rose to 5,352 but after a poor start to the season, Arthur Bunting, a former Hull K.R. player and coach, was appointed to the coaching job in January. Results improved but the club was relegated. However Bunting brought off a master stroke when he signed the experienced Steve "Knocker" Norton for £25,000 from Castleford, a deal which included Jimmy Crampton moving to Wheldon Road in an exchange deal. Sammy Lloyd also signed from Castleford and immediately broke two club records and equalled another in 1978. He beat Colin Hutton's records of 1956 by kicking 170 goals and scoring 369 points overall and he kicked 14 goals in the match against Oldham to equal Jim Kennedy's record set in 1920. Steve Norton (twice) and Vince Farrar (once) played for Great Britain against Australia. Paul Prendiville topped the try scoring list with 25 and Graham Bray scored 21. A new record unlikely to be even equalled was set up when Hull won all 26 League matches scoring 720 points and hammering Oldham 61-10 and Whitehaven 54-3. Clive Pickerill created a hat-trick of Castleford imports when he signed for a fee of £20,000. Alf Macklin was granted a ten year benefit. The average home gate was 6,853 and a working profit of £16,458 on the season was helped by a magnificent donation of £13,293 from the club's Vice-Presidents. The speedway franchise brought in £8,981. Charlie Stone (signed from Featherstone Rovers) and Steven Norton toured Australia, Norton playing in three tests. Going through Customs in Sydney, officers asked Charlie Stone to open his case and were met with the retort "it's taken me all morning to pack and close the thing ... if thee wants to see in it, thee open it and then thee try to close the thing" - needless to say, the case stayed unopened!

Vince Farrar, another signing from Featherstone Rovers, was club Captain in 1979 when Tim Wilby, Charlie Birdsall, Paul Woods, Graham Walters and Trevor Skerrett were signed on. A full house of 18,500 paid nearly £17,000 to see Hull defeat Hull K.R. 13-3 in the final of the BBC T.V. Floodlit Trophy. The average home gate was 10,021.

1976

Back Row (l. to r.): Mick Crane, Bill Ramsey, Mick Kendle, Chris Davidson, Allan Wardell, Keith Boxall, Malcolm Walker, Tony Salmon, Tony Duke, Nick Trotter, David Doyle-Davidson (Coach).
Front Row: Kenny Foulkes, Paul Hunter, George Clark, Steve Portz, Brian Hancock (Capt.), Alf Macklin, Peter Flanagan, Jack Kinsey (Baggage Man).

Keith Hepworth sees the gap in the Castleford cover. Floodlit Trophy semi-final, December 1976.

Sammy Lloyd

Referee Lindop confirms Tim Wilby's try in the 1980 R.L. Cup Final while Paul Prendiville and John Newlove show their delight. Rovers' Len Casey looks bemused.

Vince Farrar, Keith Tindall and Charlie Stone celebrate winning the 1979 Second Division Championship with coach Arthur Bunting.

In a day the city of Hull will never forget and the whole of the Rugby League marvelled at, Hull and Hull Kingston Rovers met in the Challenge Cup final at Wembley. The Robins were victorious this time, winning 10-5 in an undistingished match but red and white and black and white bedecked supporters mixed freely before, during and after the match and in a true sporting spirit. Both teams received a tremendous welcome back to the city the next day. The Colts side won their League and a profit of £22,000 was announced despite major ground improvements being carried out at the Boulevard. Travelling expenses jumped to £32,656, seat passes brought in £12,151 and the speedway franchise was increased to £10,984. Keith Boxall was granted a benefit. Retired members of staff Cyril Fowler and Bob Watson died during the season. 75,000 match programmes were produced for the twenty-four matches.

A MAGNIFICENT START TO THE 1980's

New Zealand internationals Dane O'Hara and James Leuluai were contracted in 1980 and other players signed included Bob Gaitley, Barry Banks, Ian Madley, Tony Dean, Graham Evans and Dave Topliss, while Clive Sullivan and Mike Crane re-joined the club. A new First Division attendance record was reached - the twenty-third successive five figure gate at the Boulevard and a record Premiership Final crowd of 29,448 watched the match with Hull K.R. at Headingley when the East Hull side won 11-7. It had been the sixth all-Hull final since 1920 but pace proved the vital factor - Rovers had it, Hull didn't, but Steve Norton and Tony Dean starred for Hull. The club's average home gate was a massive 11,711 and a First Division record attendance of 18,500 were at the Boulevard for the game against Hull K.R. played on Good Friday. New Zealand triumphed over Hull 33-10 at Boothferry Park. Roy Waudby, F.C.A., was elected Club Chairman. The Colts won their League and Challenge Cup. Lee Crooks won the Jim Challinor Memorial Trophy as man of the match in the Cup Final and Wayne Procter signed professional forms for the club. A profit of £60,110 was made on the year, the largest in the club's history. The freehold land and buildings at the Boulevard were now valued at £273,000 and over £100,000 was spent on ground alterations. Season passes brought in £34,468. Paul Prendiville was top try scorer with 15 and Sammy Lloyd kicked 79 goals. Vince Farrar retired and players leaving the Boulevard included Paul Woods, Ian Crowther, Charlie Birdsall and Graham

Dane O'Hara

76

Dave Topliss

Evans. Trevor Skerrett (twice) and Steve Norton (once) played for Great Britain against New Zealand.

1981 was one of the most successful seasons in the long and illustrious history of the Hull Football Club, culminating in the Rugby League Challenge Cup being won. The club had reached Wembley for the fourth time when they met cup kings Widnes. It looked odds-on that Hull would fail again at Wembley when Wright intercepted a Hull pass almost on his own line, raced down the wing and despite a late challenge from right wing Dane O'Hara, touched down to give Widnes a 14-6 lead. All looked doomed until a Steve Norton special which was converted pulled it back to 14-11 and then with little time remaining a break by substitute Lee Crooks created a gap and he put O'Hara in at the corner to level the scores at 14-14, the goal-kick was missed and so a replay was scheduled at Elland Road, Leeds, eighteen days later. Veterans Clive Sullivan and Tony Duke were called into the team which gained an 18-9 victory in an emotion charged evening before a

May 1982. We've Won the Cup!
Steve Evans, Skipper Dave Topliss, Clive Sullivan and Paul Prendiville celebrate at Elland Road after the Challenge Cup replay.

crowd of 41,711. Dave Topliss received the cup, the first Hull Captain to be on the winning side in a Challenge Cup Final since the 1913/14 season. Earlier in the season, New Zealanders Garry Kemble, Dane O'Hara and James Leuluai played together for the first time in a 42-24 win over Castleford before a crowd of 16,157. Clive Pickerill and Graham Walters had moved to Wakefield Trinity and a transfer fee of £70,500 was paid for Steve Evans from Featherstone Rovers. Steve created a unique record when he played for Featherstone against Hull K.R. in a preliminary Challenge Cup match and then received permission to turn out for Hull in the same competition, and he gained a winners' medal. A change of rule made it impossible for this to happen again. Dave Busfield was signed from Halifax for £8,000 and other new signings were Paul Wellham, Kevin Harkin, Jimmy Portz and Shaun Patrick, while Clive Sullivan re-signed. Lee Crooks was selected as Captain of the first-ever England Colts side to tour Australia. 25,165 packed into Headingley to see Hull beat Hull K. R. 12-4 in the John Player

Trevor Skerrett, Ron Wileman, Charlie Stone, Mick Crane, Sammy Lloyd, Steve Norton and sub. James Leuluai, walking out at Wembley in the 1982 Challenge Cup Final.

Trophy and Trevor Skerrett was judged man of the match. The club's average home gate was 13,190 and a new record aggregate crowd for Division One was set with 197,844 watching the fifteen matches at the Boulevard. Steve Norton reached one hundred tries in his career in the match against Castleford and he was also judged Trumann's First Division Player of the Year. The club's coach Arthur Bunting won the Trumann's Coach of the Year award. Widnes beat Hull 23-8 in the Premiership Final at Headingley. The Colts also had an outstanding season, winning their League, Challenge Cup and Premiership Final and Shaun Patrick won the Dave Valentine Memorial Trophy as man of the match in the Colts Premiership Final. Forty-five matches were played in the season and only seven were lost. Top scorers were Terry Day (19 tries), Paul Prendiville (18), Lee Crooks (115 goals) and Sammy Lloyd (64 goals). A profit of £9,512 was made on the season. Mick Dooley was appointed Secretary. Trevor Skerrett and Steve Norton played twice for Great Britain against France.

Hull came up with a revolutionary idea in 1982 to run another team in the rugby league and proposed the pre-amalgamation name of Hull White Star but the idea was turned down by the authorities. Patrick Solal was signed on and became the first top French Rugby League player to play in English Rugby League. Paul Rose was signed from Hull K.R. for £30,000, Keith Bridges from Bradford Northern for £15,000, Phil Edmonds from Hull K.R. for £10,000. Mick Harrison re-joined the club from Leeds and Andy Dannatt signed professional forms. Hull won the race to sign BARLA star Garry Schofield and also captured Gary Divorty and Neil

Tony Dean shows off the Challenge Cup on Hull's Guildhall balcony.

Puckering. Arthur Bunting was voted Trumann's Coach of the Year for the second successive year. A record first division crowd of 20,569 was achieved at the Boulevard in the derby match against Hull K.R. The Yorkshire Cup was won for the third time in the club's history when they beat Bradford Northern 18-7 and Mick Crane won the White Rose Man of the Match Trophy. The "Airlie Birds" won through to Wembley for the third time in four years and as reigning cup holders they were the strongest favourites in years to lift the trophy but Featherstone Rovers had different ideas and they won 14-12 with a late penalty goal. Paul Rose became the first player to be "sin binned" at Wembley. The Championship was won for the first time in twenty-five years, but Widnes beat them 22-10 in the Premiership Final. The Colts won their League and also their Premiership Final.

Gary Kemble

The first team gave the Australian tourists one of their hardest matches on tour when in a hard but exciting game the Aussies won 13-7. Record receipts of £29,058 were taken at this floodlit match. Despite all this success the average home gate dropped to 11,525 and a loss of £49,276 was made on the year. Season passes, including car parking, brought in £72,519. Leading scorers were Lee Crooks (113 goals 11 tries and 2 drop goals, a total of 261 points), Steve Evans 27 tries, and Dave Topliss 24 tries. The 'sin bin' was introduced on January the 1st, and Hull's

1983
Back Row (l. to r.): Trevor Skerrett, Terry Day, Phil Edmonds, Lee Crooks, Tim Wilby,
Steve Norton.
Middle Row: Paul Rose, Dane O'Hara, Barry Banks, Keith Bridges, Steve Evans, Gary Kemble,
Wayne Proctor, Mick Crane.
Front Row: Tony Duke, Tony Dean, Kevin Harkin, Dave Topliss, Charlie Stone, Paul
Prendiville, James Leuluai.

Peter Sterling

1984
Peter Sterling re-signs watched by Club Chairman, Roy Waudby.

first player to serve in the 'cooling off' period was Lee Crooks in the home match against Halifax on 16th January. Trevor Skerrett, Steve Evans and Lee Crooks (twice), Paul Rose, Dave Topliss and Steve Norton (once) played for Great Britain against Australia in the Test Series. A close season tour of Australia was not fully representative of the club's playing staff and results were disastrous.

A loss of £64,273 was recorded during the 1983 season. Garry Schofield had a great first season in senior rugby league and scored 37 tries and kicked 57 goals. He was the youngest-ever Great Britain Tourist when he was selected to tour Australia along with clubmates Lee Crooks and Wayne Proctor, while Dick Gemmell went on the management side. The Yorkshire Cup was won for the second successive year when Hull beat Castleford 13-2 at Elland Road, Leeds. A major coup was the capture of Australian Peter Sterling and not since Billy Batten's day has a player had so much influence on the club's playing record. He was ideally suited to open up play under the new six-tackle rule which had been introduced and a try was now worth four points. A new first division record was set with 147 tries and 831 points. James Leuluai scored 23 tries and Steve Evans went over for 22. Players were on the move - Terry Day to Warrington, Paul Prendiville to Leeds and Charlie Stone to Featherstone Rovers - all on one year contracts. Ron Wileman moved to Doncaster and a trio of players moved to Carlisle: Gary Peacham, Mick Sutton and Karl Portz. Kevin Harkin retired from the game and Jon Sharp and Alan Tomlinson signed on. New Zealander Fred Ah Kuoi joined Hull from North Sydney but the average home attendance dropped again, to 10,679. Three big wins were gained, over Wakefield Trinity (66-12), Salford (58-6) and Whitehaven (54-0).

Three cup finals were reached in 1984. In the first one, Hull won the Yorkshire Cup for the third successive season when they beat local rivals Hull K.R. 29-12 at

Steve Evans slides in for Hull's second try in the 1985 Challenge Cup Final against Wigan at Wembley.

James Leuluai touches down for Hull's fifth try in the 1985 Challenge Cup Final against Wigan at Wembley.

Lee Crooks

Boothferry Park. Scrum half Peter Sterling won the White Rose Man of the Match Trophy. The "Robins" had their revenge later in the season when they beat Hull 12-0 in the John Player Trophy Final at Boothferry Park.

For the fourth time in six years Hull reached Wembley and it was the game's 50th Final there. Wigan were the opponents and it proved to be one of the greatest finals and a magnificent advertisement for the game of rugby league. Hull went into an early lead but Wigan came back strongly, inspired by Lance Todd Trophy winner Brett Kenny and they went into a 28-12 lead. Hull pulled back to 28-24 but they had left it too late. Hull fielded a record six overseas players - Sterling, O'Hara, Leuluai, Ah Kuoi, Kemble and John Muggleton, (Sterling's brother-in-law who was signed from Paramatta).

Earlier on in the season Kevin James was signed from the Welsh R.U. side Aberavon while on the move were Barry Banks to Hunslet and Dave Topliss to Oldham on a free transfer. Clive Sullivan joined Doncaster as player/coach. Lee Crooks was voted young player of the year and Andrew Kamis was judged Dave Valentine Memorial Trophy winner in the Colts Premiership Final against Leigh. The 'A' team won their Challenge Cup Final beating Hunslet 28-10. The first team beat Workington Town 64-18 to register their highest ever away victory, and Carlisle were beaten 52-6. Top scorers were Steve Evans (24 tries), Garry Schofield (23 tries, 104 goals and one drop goal, a total of 301 points) and Dane O'Hara (22 tries). ABI Caravans of Beverley signed a jersey sponsorship with the club. The average home gate dropped again, this time to 8,525. Former Chairman Charles Watson died after a car crash.

Garry Schofield scored 15 tries, 35 goals and one drop goal to total 131 points in the 1985 season while Dane O'Hara touched down 19 times and Lee Crooks kicked 52 goals. Paul Prendiville scored the 100th try of his career at York in September. Oldham were thrashed 54-12. Lee Crooks, Shaun Patrick and Friend, Tamati and Filipanino were sent off in the tour match against New Zealand. The Kiwis won 33-10 before a crowd of 8406. The club's average gate was 6,245, the third highest in the Rugby League, behind Leeds and Wigan. Kenny Foulkes was put in charge temporarily as club coach between December 1985 and May 1986. St. Helens scored 57 points against Hull, the highest number of points ever scored against the Black and Whites.

John Rawlings took over as Chairman of the club and Garry Schofield was the club's top scorer in 1986 with 32 tries while Welsh R.U. signing Gary Pearce totalled 148 points although he only played periodically. The Colts won their League and the 'A' team won the Alliance Cup. Len Casey was appointed club coach on a two year contract, replacing Arthur Bunting who had been a most successful coach and the club made him an honorary life member. A dismal playing record resulted in relegation only being avoided in the last match of the season when Hull beat Widnes at the Boulevard and Oldham went down to the Second Division instead. Captain Lee Crooks was transferred to Leeds for a world record fee of £150,000 - a move most fans deprecated but the club said their financial position was such they needed the cash and so Crooks had to go to help solve the problem. The club's average home gate was 5,538, fourth in the Rugby League behind Wigan, St. Helens and Leeds. The Australian tourists beat Hull 48-0 before a crowd of 8,213. Aussie prop Geoff Gerard joined the club from

Penrith. Steve Norton had a benefit season which eventually raised £41,000, a rugby league record.

More than 1,000 people packed Holy Trinity Church in Hull's Market Place for a memorial service to Clive Sullivan, who died from cancer on 8th October. The Great Britain side named their new Lion Mascot 'Sully' in his memory.

And finally, just think what a crowd these players who have worn the famous black and white irregular hoops would bring to the Boulevard:

PRE-WAR - Freddie Miller; Jack Harrison V.C., Joe Oliver, Billy Batten, Billy

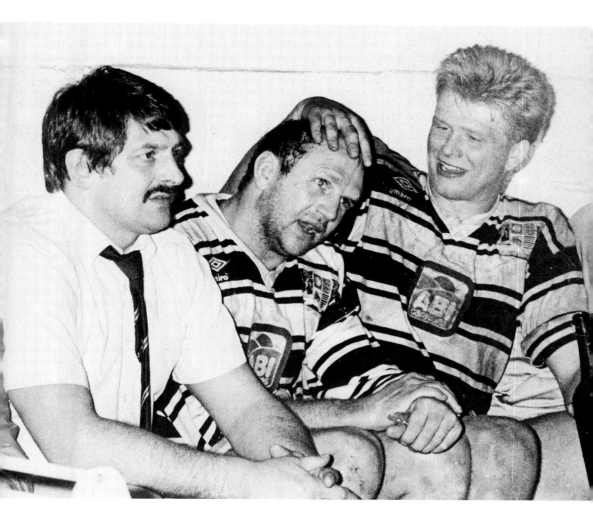

Nicky Elgar congratulates Steve Norton who had just been substituted in the final match of the season against Widnes. "Knocker" won the Man of the Match award in what was his final match for Hull before he announced his retirement. Coach Len Casey looks on.

Stone; Jimmy Deveraux, Eddie Caswell; Laurie Thacker, George Barlow, Harold Bowman, Bob Taylor, Charlie Booth and Harold Ellerington.

POST-WAR - Colin Hutton; Bruce Ryan, Garry Schofield, James Leuluai, Clive Sullivan M.B.E.; Dave Topliss, Peter Sterling; Mick Harrison, Tommy Harris, Len Casey, Lee Crooks, Steve Norton and Johnny Whiteley.

Such would be the skill and individualism on show that neither team would need a captain!

1988 UPDATE

1987/8 was certainly a season of happenings, on and off the field. After a contractual disagreement with the club, Gary Schofield was transferred to Leeds for a world record fee of £175,000. John Carroll was signed from Batley and Terry Regan, Dave Brooks and Scott Gale came from Australia with James Leuluai re-signing from Leigh.

After only one full match, Gale was injured against Leeds and he had to return to Australia. Paul McAffery was signed to replace him and Paul Fletcher was signed from Salford.

St. Helens inflicted a record 64-2 defeat on the Airlie Birds.

Hull reached the semi-final of the Challenge Cup and lost 3-4 to a late try against Halifax after a 0-0 draw.

Coach Len Casey sensationally resigned on the eve of the match and assistant Coaches Tony Dean and Keith Hepworth were given charge until the end of the Season.

Late Season victories against Halifax, Wigan, Leeds and Hull K.R. lifted the relegation gloom.

There was a remarkable finish to the Wigan match at the Boulevard. Scores were level at 12-12 when Wigan were awarded a penalty in the last minute. Joe Lydon missed the kick, which was gathered by Gary Pearce who beat Shelford, starting a near length of the field move before McAffery went in under the posts for a sensational try, goaled by Pearce and the crowd went wild. It must have been one of the most thrilling finishes ever to a match at the Boulevard.

In the final season of the Colts' set-up before re-organisation with BARLA, Hull Colts won the League and Cup and Premiership Final to complete a remarkable season.

Gary Divorty (14) and Paul Eastwood (13) topped the first team's try scoring list. Gary Pearce kicked 111 goals and scored 6 tries. The average crowd was 5,111. Brian Smith, previously coach with Australian Club IllaWara, was given a coaching contract for the 1988/9 season and he brought across David Moon, Neil Henry, Craig Coleman and David Boyle from Australia.

Local lad Stan Pickering was appointed assistant coach and Mike Stanley became Hon. Secretary. Harry Markham and Bob Kavanagh, former Hull players, died in 1988.

SHOPACHECK WERE THE CLUB'S MAIN SPONSORS FOR SEASON 1988/9
Hull F.C.'s sponsor launch at the Boulevard with trophies for the 'player of the season' and
'young player of the season' as well as a 'supporter of the season' award
(Left to right) Sandy Muir (joint managing director of Shopacheck), Dane O'Hara,
Brian Smith (new manager), Gary Pearce and John Rawlings (Hull FC chairman)

BIBLIOGRAPHY

Hull F.C. Centenary Booklet   R.E. Lee and J.A. Saville 1965

The History of Rugby League   Brochure issued to coincide with an exhibition organised by the International Rugby League Supporters Federation and Kingston upon Hull City Council at Hull Town Docks Museum. 1979

Rothman's Rugby League
Yearbooks 1981 to 1987   Raymond Fletcher and David Howes

Hull and Rovers through 88
Seasons   Christopher Elton 1981

The Yorkshire Athletic Annual   "Chasseur" 1898

Hull F.C. Annual Reports 1881 - 1987

The "Hull Daily Mail" and "Hull and Yorkshire Times", the "Yorkshire Post"
and various other newspapers.

APPEARANCES AND SCORERS 1895-96 to 1987-88

The following is a list of all players to have appeared in the Hull F.C. first team since the formation of the Northern Union in September 1895. Only Competitive games are included in the record (i.e. League games, Cup-Ties and national touring sides, although abandoned matches and those replayed for any reason are also included). Following common practice, and guidance from the Rugby Football League and the Rugby League Record Keepers Club, those games played in 1915-16 to December 1918 are not included as these games were not part of any properly constituted competitions. However, League and Cup games in the Second World War are included. Where a guest player turned out for Hull, this is indicated by his normal club appearing in brackets. (Where known).

The debut date is indicated in all cases, but it should be noted that many of the players involved in the early days of the Northern Union actually played for Hull prior to the Northern Union being founded. I have used the first appearance in the Northern Union as the debut date.

Player	Debut Date	App.(sub)		Tries	Goals	Points
Abbott. (Hunslet)	4.09.1943	6		0	0	0
Abey. J.	27.09.1969	5		0	0	0
Adamson. W.	25.02.1897	9		3	0	9
Adamson.	4.10.1930	30		2	0	6
Ah Kuoi. F.	2.10.1983	116	(10)	28	1Drop	113
Ainley.	11.03.1944	1		0	0	0
Akester. H.	16.09.1922	23		7	0	21
Allen. A.	2.09.1911	70		11	0	33
Allen. A.E.	8.10.1938	131		31	10	113
Ali. C.	3.01.1959	24		8	0	24
(Later C. Mountain)						
Anderson. W.	5.09.1907	219		16	13	74
Anderson.	12.01.1946	8		0	0	0
Appleyard. M.	19.10.1907	4		1	0	3
Armitt. T. (Swinton)	20.02.1943	20		0	0	0
Arnett. C.	30.09.1984	10	(8)	3	0	9
Ashbridge. G.	22.11.1958	4		1	0	3
Ashton. J.	15.11.1930	11		2	0	6
Aston. H.	5.02.1972	14	(3)	1	0	3
Atkinson. B.	7.11.1925	8		0	0	0
Atkinson. H.	28.01.1905	24		5	0	15
Atkinson. H.	5.09.1925	10		3	0	9
Atkinson. S. (HKR)	6.03.1943	20		5	0	15
Bancroft. A.	11.11.1977	1		0	0	0
Banham. A.	29.11.1974	21	(7)	11	0	33
Banks. B.	12.10.1980	80	(18)	24	0	74
Banks. S.J.	29.09.1906	27		2	1	8
Barham. R.	15.03.1975	5		0	0	0
Barker. G.E.	7.09.1895	23		4	1Pen.	15
Barker. J.S.	21.09.1895	56		1	2Drop	11
Barlow. G.H.	25.10.1930	274		18	0	54
Barlow. L.	5.03.1934	173		27	0	81

Player	Debut Date	App.(sub)		Tries	Goals	Points
Barnwell. K.	26.08.1961	43	(1)	13	0	39
Barr. K.	26.01.1975	20	(2)	2	0	6
Barraclough. H.	20.10.1900	6		0	0	0
Barrow. A.	9.11.1911	29		7	1	23
Barton. J.	8.09.1906	1		0	0	0
Bateman. G.W.	20.09.1933	178		123	0	369
Bateson. A.E.	29.09.1923	282		73	241	701
Bateson. P.	17.08.1957	138		5	542	1099
Batten. E.	4.12.1920	3		2	0	6
Batten. W. (Billy)	12.04.1913	226		89	1	269
Batten. W. (Jnr)	22.01.1927	16		1	0	3
Battersby. F.	8.10.1910	22		6	5	28
Baxter. L.	12.09.1942	53		6	0	18
Baxter. R.	24.12.1932	1		0	0	0
Beales. G.	3.09.1938	44		2	0	6
Beales. W.	18.11.1911	5		3	0	15
Beaumont. H. (HKR)	13.09.1941	9		0	0	0
Beaumont. J.	21.10.1899	1		0	0	0
Beaumont. L. (HKR)	13.09.1941	57		6	0	0
Beardshaw. H.	22.11.1924	64		16	27	102
Beasley. J.	19.01.1969	2		0	0	0
Beasty. J.	25.12.1912	283		14	0	0
Bedford. A.	5.09.1946	208		21	0	63
Bedford. E. (HKR)	12.09.1942	32		5	0	15
(later transferred to Hull in 1947-48)						
Bedford. H.	2.09.1939	20		2	0	6
Bell. A.	9.01.1983	-	(1)	0	0	0
Bell. F.J.	19.01.1901	17		0	0	0
Bell. R.	9.01.1965	2		0	0	0
Bell. T.	5.01.1907	12		6	0	18
Bemrose. W.O.	6.04.1912	1		0	0	0
Benson. E.L.	15.04.1926	9		5	0	15
Bilton. J.	16.04.1938	43		7	0	21
Birdsall. C.	2.09.1979	55	(11)	17	8+2Drop	69
Blanchard. L. (HKR)	26.09.1942	1		0	0	0
Bland. W.	21.03.1904	8		2	0	6
Boagey. H.	23.08.1948	20		3	0	9
Boddy. R.	26.09.1936	9		0	0	0
Bolderson. R.W.	25.11.1922	126		2	0	6
Bolton. J.	3.04.1896	14		2	0	6
Bond.	18.09.1943	5		0	0	0
Booth. C. (Snr)	31.08.1935	336		47	1	143
Booth. C. (Jnr)	28.08.1961	85	(4)	2	0	6
Booth. G.	7.09.1895	33		2	0	6
Booth. R.	5.10.1963	66	(5)	2	0	6
Boustead. R.	11.10.1958	14		6	0	18
Bowden. J. (Bramley)	10.10.1942	1		0	0	0
Bowers. A.	26.11.1938	161		82	0	246
Bowman. H.	10.12.1921	451		75	0	225
Bowman. K.	15.08.1953	149		90	0	270
Boxall. K.	28.03.1970	285	(35)	98	209	712
Boylen. F.	3.09.1908	141		14	2	46
Bradley	12.12.1942	1		0	0	0
Brand. M.	9.04.1986	26		8	0	32
Bray. G.	6.02.1977	143		55	0	165

Player	Debut Date	App.(sub)		Tries	Goals	Points
Brennan. W.	8.09.1923	23		0	0	0
Bridges. K.	5.09.1982	29		1	0	3
Brindle. D.	16.10.1954	16		3	0	9
Britton. F.	4.03.1911	2		0	0	0
Britton. S.	3.09.1908	65		6	0	18
Broadhurst. F.	31.08.1957	121		32	0	96
Brocklebank. J.	3.10.1896	1		0	0	0
Brogden. S.	17.09.1938	84		34	19	140
Brook. A.	22.12.1928	1		0	0	0
Brooks. D.	11.10.1987	24	(1)	2	0	8
Broom. E.	1.02.1964	223	(21)	22	165	396
Brown. D.	5.10.1986	9		1	0	3
Brown. E.W.	8.03.1902	35		8	1	26
Brown. J.	19.12.1964	75	(5)	22	18	102
Brown. R.S.	9.04.1909	1		0	0	0
Brown. W.	12.11.1927	1		0	0	0
Bruce. T.	5.09.1907	42		8	64	152
Brunyard. J.	25.11.1905	8		0	1	2
Bryan. G.E.	26.12.1895	3		0	0	0
Burchell. J.W.	24.09.1904	82		11	0	33
Burnell. D.	27.08.1949	82		9	0	27
Burrell. W.	7.10.1899	2		0	0	0
Busfield. D.	17.03.1982	2	(2)	1	0	3
Butler. R.	29.11.1974	1		0	0	0
Buttery. C.H.	25.12.1899	8		0	0	0
Calder. S.	10.11.1973	3	(2)	1	0	3
Calvert.	2.04.1934	1		0	0	0
Camac. (Salford)	30.09.1944	5		1	0	3
Cambriani. A.	3.03.1985	-	(1)	0	0	0
Cappleman. C.H.	9.12.1911	44		9	3	33
Carlisle. T.	5.09.1903	35		0	0	0
Carmichael. A.	2.02.1929	244		38	0	114
Carmichael. G. (Bradford)	13.11.1943	8		3	0	9
Carmichael. T.	14.09.1963	59		11	0	33
Carr. H.R.	7.09.1895	1		0	0	0
Carroll. W.J.	26.11.1904	123		9	0	27
Carroll. J.	3.01.1988	15	(2)	0	0	0
Carvill. P.J.	24.10.1903	66		31	0	93
Casey. L.	9.09.1970	91	(11)	14	0	42
Casey. T.	11.09.1963	5		0	0	0
Castles. J.W.	14.09.1907	17		10	0	30
Caswell. E.	25.10.1919	401		98	5	304
Chapman. W. (Warrington)	5.09.1942	1		0	0	0
Charles. W.J.	19.03.1921	34		9	0	27
Charlesworth. G.	22.10.1966	13		0	0	0
Chester. R.	26.10.1980	5	(5)	2	0	6
Clark. G.	9.02.1975	87	(4)	52	0	156
Clark. J.	10.04.1950	29		2	0	6
Clark. K.	30.10.1974	9	(1)	0	0	0
Clark. L. (HKR)	6.09.1941	90		7	0	21
Clarkson. E.	1.09.1910	91		1	3	9
Clarkson. G.	4.11.1987	1		0	0	0
Clapham. (Huddersfield)	30.09.1944	1		0	0	0
Clawson. T.	2.03.1980	2		0	0	0

Player	Debut Date	App.(sub)	Tries	Goals	Points
Clixby. B.	21.04.1961	65 (7)	21	0	63
Codd. A. (HKR)	2.09.1944	6	0	0	0
Cole. C.	29.01.1955	35	4	0	12
Colling. F.	3.02.1934	82	10	0	30
Collins. T.	1.09.1923	153	52	0	156
Collinson. A.	16.09.1984	4 (1)	2	0	6
Connell. G.	19.09.1908	139	23	3	75
Conway. B.	26.02.1949	159	30	4	98
Cook. F.J.	6.09.1902	151	29	8	103
Cooper. B.	8.04.1950	106	37	0	111
Cooper. C.	8.04.1973	6 (4)	3	1	11
Corban. I.	20.01.1962	18	1	0	3
Corner. R.	3.03.1934	209	74	0	222
Cornish. F.H.	2.09.1899	12	0	0	0
Cotterill.	16.03.1933	1	0	0	0
Cottrell. G.T.	5.09.1907	204	67	0	201
Coulman. W.	16.04.1954	21	12	0	36
Coulthard. J.	12.09.1896	29	3	1Drop	13
Coupland. P.	2.09.1979	13 (4)	0	0	0
Courtney. W.J.	20.04.1929	173	16	2	52
Coverdale. R.	22.09.1951	205	13	0	39
Coverley. R.	18.05.1963	14 (1)	2	0	6
Cowan. J.	6.12.1924	19	1	0	3
Cowan. M.	11.10.1981	- (1)	0	0	0
Cowan. R.	31.03.1972	12	2	0	6
Cowan. S.	25.09.1954	163	66	0	198
Cox. G.	13.01.1951	30	16	0	48
Crampton. J.	15.02.1976	47 (1)	11	0	33
Crane. H.	3.05.1941	77	24	0	72
Crane. M.	4.12.1970	324 (35)	98	3+11Drop	311
Crawford.	6.02.1943	1	0	0	0
Croft. K.	15.01.1938	44	23	0	69
Croft.	21.11.1959	1	0	0	0
Crook.	23.04.1945	1	0	0	0
Crooks. L.	30.11.1980	196 (12)	44	389+11Drop	947
Crooks. S.	7.09.1986	34 (4)	0	1Drop	1
Crossland.	30.10.1943	10	3	0	9
Crowe. F.	1.09.1900	11	4	0	12
Crowther. I.D.	8.08.1976	36 (1)	6	0	18
Cummings. R.	27.09.1928	5	0	0	0
Curtis.	19.11.1932	6	1	0	3
Daddy. M.	11.01.1941	7	0	0	0
Dale. W.	29.01.1898	44	8	2	28
Dannatt. A.	16.01.1983	68 (29)	12	0	48
Dannatt. G.	1.09.1956	61	20	0	60
Danter. T.	30.10.1948	77	3	0	9
D'Arcy. C.	14.01.1905	15	4	1	14
Darlington. B.	7.04.1956	21	11	0	33
Darmody. S.	5.09.1912	89	16	18	84
Davidson. Chris	24.04.1964	258 (40)	86	148+9Drop	563
Davidson. Colin	26.04.1973	1	0	0	0
Davies. D.	1.02.1964	8	0	0	0
Davies. E.R.	6.09.1947	10	0	0	0
Davies. P.	26.09.1953	1	0	0	0

Player	Debut Date	App.(sub)		Tries	Goals	Points
Davies. R.W.	19.12.1936	29		13	0	39
Davies. W.J.	17.01.1925	217		49	17	181
Dawson. J.R.P.	16.04.1932	239		26	0	78
Day. T.	8.11.1981	53	(6)	31	0	113
Deacon. N.	11.10.1895	1		0	0	0
Dean. A.	15.03.1981	53	(9)	14	9Drop	52
Deane. S.	12.09.1914	21		4	0	12
Dechan. J.	3.09.1908	29		17	0	51
Deere. J.A.	17.02.1900	3		0	0	0
Dennison. S.	11.11.1979	29	(7)	7	41	103
Desborough. A.	11.01.1947	11		0	0	0
Devereux. J.	20.03.1909	181		101	4	311
Devonshire. T.	16.04.1960	325	(9)	123	1	371
Dick. K.	21.09.1986	32	(10)	5	3+1Drop	27
Dickinson. W.H.	15.11.1923	5		0	0	0
Dinsdale. J.	1.11.1919	1		0	0	0
Dinsdale. T.	29.10.1910	8		2	0	6
Dittmar. L.	20.10.1972	18		6	0	18
Divorty. G.	28.08.1983	114	(28)	34	17+10Drop	180
Dockar. A. (HKR)	31.03.1945	1		0	0	0
Dockar. W.	11.04.1938	128		87	0	261
Donkin. L.	28.09.1895	53		1	0	3
Downing. W.	13.11.1943	9		0	0	0
Doyle-Davidson. D.	18.02.1961	158	(25)	23	1	71
Drake. J.G.	26.03.1951	245		38	1	116
Drake. W.D.	11.04.1953	295		101	53	409
Drew. A.	15.12.1972	1	(2)	0	0	0
Driscoll. J.	17.09.1898	87		24	1	74
Duffield. G.	18.02.1908	1		0	0	0
Duffy. P.	12.02.1910	3		0	0	0
Duke. A.	23.03.1968	214	(1)	18	0	54
Dunn. T.	8.09.1900	3		0	1	2
Dusher. T.	29.11.1974	1		0	0	0
Eaton. C. (Leeds)	6.02.1943	1		1	0	3
Eastburn. M.	29.09.1928	29		1	0	3
Eastwood. J. (HKR)	26.12.1942	1		0	0	0
Eastwood. J.	6.03.1988	1		0	0	0
Eastwood. P.	3.02.1985	104	(5)	47	2	184
Eddoms. J.(Wakefield)	19.09.1942	11		0	0	0
Edmonds. J. (HKR)	26.12.1942	12		5	0	15
Edmonds. P.	9.01.1983	75	(9)	24	0	92
Edmonds. R.	12.01.1973	18	(7)	2	0	6
Edmunds. D.H.	16.01.1904	5		0	0	0
Edson. J.	18.05.1964	68	(6)	1	0	3
Edwards.	20.10.1945	1		0	0	0
Eggett. C.W.	23.01.1907	8		2	0	6
Eley. W.	2.02.1898	7		1	0	3
Elgar. N.	11.03.1987	17	(3)	3	0	12
Ellerington. G.	13.09.1902	30		2	0	6
Ellerington. H.	1.03.1930	268		53	2	160
Ellery. C.E.	25.08.1923	19		5	0	15
Elliott. D.	10.05.1981	11	(1)	2	0	6
Ellis. B.	16.05.1964	2		0	0	0
Ellis. I.	11.10.1987	4	(4)	3	0	12

Player	Debut Date	App.(sub)	Tries	Goals	Points
Ellis. J.	19.03.1921	39	0	0	0
Empson. G.W.	13.02.1912	10	4	1	11
Errington. S.	22.01.1927	141	6	0	18
Evans. G.	19.08.1979	35 (5)	10	0	30
Evans. H.	10.01.1948	94	17	6	63
Evans. L.G.	5.09.1903	21	2	1	8
Evans. Sam.	26.09.1959	17	2	1	8
Evans. Steve.	7.02.1982	136 (5)	90	16	351
Everitt. R.G.	24.03.1928	38	4	0	12
Fallon. P.	9.11.1946	21	1	0	3
Farrar. V.	23.11.1977	86 (6)	10	0	30
Fearnley. W.	2.10.1897	27	3	8	27
Feetham. W.	7.09.1895	70	2	0	6
Fifield. C.R.	21.11.1931	224	80	13	266
Fildes. P.	29.01.1898	124	13	0	39
Finn. T.	4.12.1954	374	131	1	395
Firth. H.	5.08.1968	138	56	0	168
Firth. R.	9.11.1968	75 (1)	2	0	6
Fisher. A.	28.11.1903	1	0	0	0
Flanagan. P.	21.10.1975	20 (1)	2	0	6
Fleming. M.W.	27.12.1919	6	1	0	3
Fletcher. P.	30.08.1987	34	8	0	24
Fletcher. T.	19.09.1936	29	0	38	76
Foreman. D.	9.09.1950	76	7	14	49
Forrester.	15.02.1919	5	0	0	0
Forshaw. R.	6.11.1897	58	14	0	42
Forster. C.	10.11.1967	69 (6)	1	0	3
Foster. L.	2.03.1974	3 (1)	1	0	3
Foulkes. K.	10.10.1964	228 (23)	27	4	89
Francis. A.	1.09.1910	247	166	2	502
Francis. R.	12.11.1949	127	60	0	180
Franklin. G.E.	15.02.1913	1	0	0	0
Franks. D.	11.09.1897	153	31	8	109
Frater. J.	7.09.1901	2	0	0	0
Freear. A.E.	1.10.1904	61	19	0	57
French. J.	6.01.1945	4	0	0	0
Fulton. H.	7.09.1901	209	11	0	33
Gaitley. R.	5.10.1980	15 (5)	5	9Drop	24
Gale. S.	4.10.1987	4	1	0	4
Galloway. D.	1.09.1910	31	2	0	6
Gardiner. J.	3.01.1927	35	5	1	17
Garmston. F.	20.11.1948	10	0	0	0
Garratt. F.	28.10.1922	3	0	0	0
Garratt. H.	25.01.1919	212	67	0	201
Garvey. R.	26.09.1925	13	4	0	12
Gascoigne. A.	1.09.1985	24 (3)	7	0	28
Gee.	25.03.1944	1	0	0	0
Gemmell. R.	19.08.1961	151 (1)	36	0	108
Geraghty. A.	11.04.1970	57 (11)	3	7	23
Gerrard.	3.09.1938	1	0	0	0
Gerrard. G.	18.09.1985	22 (2)	6	0	24
Gibbins. M.	21.09.1986	3 (1)	0	0	0
Gibbons. A.	28.10.1972	19 (2)	4	0	12

Player	Debut Date	App.(sub)	Tries	Goals	Points
Gilbert. H.	5.09.1912	114	57	1	173
Gill. R.	11.10.1958	18	3	0	9
Gill. W.	21.11.1895	6	0	0	0
Gillard. N.	10.10.1966	1	0	0	0
Gillyon.	4.10.1930	15	0	0	0
Gissing.	27.08.1932	6	0	0	0
Gittoes. K.	23.09.1948	123	41	0	123
Glynn.T.	28.03.1942	137	39	0	117
Goddard. R.T.	6.09.1902	95	6	33	84
Golby. J.(Featherstone)	10.10.1942	1	0	0	0
Goodall. W.	18.09.1937	15	2	0	6
Goodfellow. F.J.	3.09.1904	54	8	66	156
Gorman. F.	6.11.1897	95	8	0	24
Gouldstone. C.G.	31.08.1935	31	19	0	57
Grady. J.	25.08.1923	9	0	0	0
Graham. T. (Huddersfield)	7.10.1944	2	0	0	0
Greenwood. W.	22.02.1913	7	0	0	0
Gresswell. J.R.	24.01.1920	8	0	0	0
Grice. A.	23.09.1911	180	31	0	93
Griffin. D.	31.03.1985	1 (1)	0	0	0
Griffin. W.	30.11.1895	10	3	0	9
Gutherless.	5.02.1944	1	0	0	0
Gwynne. T.E.	10.09.1921	284	107	0	321
Hagan.	26.09.1942	6	1	2	8
Halafihi. N.	9.01.1960	21	6	0	18
Hall. G.	6.09.1902	85	12	0	36
Hall. P.	20.03.1977	9 (7)	0	3	6
Hall. W.	2.09.1905	20	1	0	3
Hall. Wilson	3.09.1927	44	2	0	6
Hambling. B.	31.08.1957	103	16	0	48
Hambrecht. A.	7.09.1901	26	7	0	21
Hamm. B.	1.09.1900	14	1	0	3
Hammill. J.	4.10.1913	57	24	6	84
Hancock. B.	8.04.1967	396 (15)	107	8+17Drop	354
Hand. L.	24.05.1947	9	1	0	3
Hardaker. J.	4.01.1902	4	0	0	0
Hargreaves. W.	21.11.1903	59	3	0	9
Harkin. K.	8.11.1981	61 (8)	19	0	60
Harland. P.	30.09.1911	7	0	0	0
Harmer. W.	7.09.1895	138	9	0	27
Harris. C.E.	13.09.1924	8	4	0	12
Harris. P.T.	21.01.1950	443	56	2	172
Harrison. A.	16.01.1904	24	3	0	9
Harrison. C.	17.09.1978	44 (5)	17	0	51
Harrison. F.	12.10.1895	1	0	0	0
Harrison. G.	21.08.1957	45	23	0	69
Harrison. Jack.	5.09.1912	101	91	2	277
Harrison. James.	6.09.1902	147	1	9	21
Harrison. Jim.	30.04.1971	19 (6)	2	0	6
Harrison. M.	16.08.1965	318 (3)	15	0	45
Harrison. R.	17.10.1931	7	1	0	3
Harrison. S.	27.12.1949	7	1	0	3
Harsley. R.	20.10.1928	51	9	0	27
Hart. T.	20.11.1948	141	11	281	595

Player	Debut Date	App.(sub)	Tries	Goals	Points
Hattersley. S.	7.01.1939	150	12	0	36
Hatfield. H.	24.09.1898	3	0	0	0
Havelock. H.	10.09.1908	31	2	0	6
Hayes.	26.11.1949	2	0	0	0
Heath. L.V.	1.04.1911	1	0	1	2
Hemingway. M.	26.04.1973	1	0	0	0
Henderson.	25.12.1957	1	0	0	0
Henrikson. E.	13.04.1925	3	0	0	0
Hepworth. K.	5.10.1976	58 (3)	11	2	37
Herberts. E.	24.03.1934	213	74	6	234
Herridge. T.	5.09.1907	379	46	1	140
Hewson. H.	4.09.1920	8	0	0	0
Hick. S.	31.03.1985	18 (6)	2	10	28
Hicks. M.	1.10.1972	24	8	0	24
Higginbottom.	13.09.1941	1	0	0	0
Higgins. W.	5.09.1912	26	6	1	20
Higham. F.	5.11.1898	9	0	0	0
Higo. J.	24.10.1925	19	0	0	0
Hilson. J.	6.12.1924	4	1	0	3
Hockley. N.	10.01.1953	121	14	0	42
Hodgson. D.	3.04.1977	- (1)	0	0	0
Hodgson. W.	12.09.1896	34	4	8	28
Hogg. R.	11.12.1937	38	4	0	12
Holden. J.H.	11.01.1913	7	0	4	8
Holder. W.	5.09.1907	293	30	3	96
Holdstock. A.	25.08.1954	41	7	0	21
Holdsworth. J.	13.04.1914	158	69	2	141
Holgate. M.	22.08.1959	3	4	3	18
Holliday. J.A.	11.04.1914	17	1	0	3
Hollindrake. T.	15.10.1960	114	49	28	203
Holmes. J.	7.09.1895	33	4	0	12
Holt. A.	11.12.1971	13 (1)	0	0	0
Holt. J.	7.09.1940	62	10	0	30
Homan. B.	5.10.1895	10	0	0	0
Hooton.	26.09.1942	2	0	0	0
Hopkins. W.J.	8.04.1950	40	0	0	0
Hopper. A.	22.02.1898	2	1	0	3
Howlett. G.	31.12.1921	91	15	0	45
Hufton. J.	3.09.1904	40	1	0	3
Hughes. F.	14.01.1911	21	2	0	6
Huggins. P.	23.02.1952	1	0	0	0
Hulme. J.	18.01.1919	27	3	2	13
Humphries. J.	4.09.1920	28	8	0	24
Hunter. P.	5.01.1975	61 (5)	17	5	61
Hurley. F.	17.04.1937	67	29	0	87
Hutchins.	6.09.1941	1	0	0	0
Hutton. C.	10.03.1951	262	23	628	1325
Huxley. K.	15.08.1964	105 (19)	31	4	101
Ibbertson. P.	26.11.1968	58 (23)	5	0	15
Ingram. P.	19.10.1940	91	12	4	44
Jacketts. G.	7.09.1895	64	3	1 Pen.	12
Jackson. D.	25.08.1947	81	6	0	18

Player	Debut Date	App.(sub)		Tries	Goals	Points
Jackson. L.	16.04.1986	11	(2)	1	0	3
Jackson. R.W.	8.11.1902	40		12	12	60
Jacklin. R.	10.02.1974	6		1	0	3
Jacques. W.	7.09.1895	122		32	137	370
James. K.	30.09.1984	33	(3)	17	0	68
Jeffries.	1.12.1945	15		9	0	27
Jenkins. E.	6.09.1902	56		15	1	47
Jenkins. J.	1.11.1958	4		0	0	0
Jenney. E.	15.03.1924	257		6	38	94
Jervis. D.	2.09.1968	15	(4)	1	0	3
Jewitt. R.	15.09.1945	61		21	1	65
Jimmeson. S,	16.03.1946	80		3	0	9
John T.	8.02.1902	27		0	0	0
Johnson. C.H.	15.12.1900	14		2	0	6
Johnson. D.	16.01.1960	35		15	0	45
Johnson. F.	24.08.1963	29	(1)	2	0	6
Johnson. T.A.	10.10.1936	128		21	1	65
Johnson. W.	7.09.1895	77		3	1+1Drop	15
Johnson. W.	27.12.1919	3		0	0	0
Jones.	2.04.1932	3		2	0	6
Jones.	29.01.1944	1		0	0	0
Jones. E.W.	20.01.1906	19		4	1	14
Jones. J.	14.03.1925	1		0	0	0
Jones. J.M.	3.09.1908	23		2	0	6
Jones. J.R.	10.02.1945	16		4	0	12
Jones. L.	3.04.1971	1		0	1	2
Jones. W.G.	5.02.1949	22		0	1	2
Joy.	20.04.1946	1		1	0	3
Kavanagh. R.	11.10.1938	78		7	0	21
Kear. B.	27.01.1974	13	(3)	2	0	6
Keegan. A.	13.12.1958	363	(1)	31	318	729
Kelsey. E.C.	19.01.1901	1		0	0	0
Kemble. G.	30.08.1981	190	(5)	45	1	162
Kendle. M.	11.09.1971	63	(3)	5	132	279
Kennedy. J.E.	9.01.1915	237		68	523	1250
Kennedy. W.	18.01.1919	19		4	0	12
Kerman. R.	15.03.1987	2	(1)	0	0	0
Kershaw. J.	14.12.1957	86		13	1	41
Kew. G.	25.10.1913	1		0	0	0
Kielty. B.	13.04.1957	1		0	0	0
Kilburn. G.	3.09.1904	140		9	2	31
Kilby. A.	11.04.1970	2		0	0	0
Kirby. R.	18.09.1897	13		0	0	0
Kirchin. T.	9.08.1969	118	(2)	19	0	57
Kirk. W.H.	23.04.1910	4		0	0	0
Kirkwood. J.	26.10.1986	-	(1)	0	0	0
Knapp. C.	9.12.1950	31		2	0	6
Lamping. John	25.04.1925	6		0	0	0
Lamping. Joseph	25.04.1925	1		0	0	0
Land. A.	7.04.1906	1		0	0	0
Lane. S.	29.11.1974	18	(2)	2	0	6
Langfield. G.	3.10.1953	10		2	4	14

Player	Debut Date	App.(sub)	Tries	Goals	Points
Langhorn. W.	13.09.1902	82	0	0	0
Larkins. C.W.	21.01.1905	14	1	0	3
Larvin.	23.10.1930	1	0	0	0
Lawrence. E.	24.09.1938	265	58	3	180
Lawson.	20.03.1943	10	0	1	2
Lawson. J.	13.04.1953	9	0	0	0
Lazenby. C.	5.10.1976	28 (19)	7	10	41
Lazenby. T.	16.11.1986	13 (3)	2	0	8
Lempriere. C.C.	7.09.1895	138	56	1	170
Leuluai. J.	27.09.1981	178 (5)	85	0	309
Lewis. G.H.	10.10.1903	51	0	0	0
Lewis. J.	6.09.1902	127	7	0	21
Lewis. S.	7.09.1901	4	0	0	0
Lloyd. G.	20.08.1978	103 (18)	20	366+1Drop	793
Lockwood.J.S.	10.12.1910	2	1	0	3
Lofthouse. W.	12.10.1896	14	3	0	9
Longbottom. H.	22.11.1924	82	2	0	6
Loveluck. W.R.	19.01.1924	23	3	0	9
Low. C.A.	3.10.1896	34	3	0	9
Lowery. W.A.	25.12.1899	10	1	0	3
Lunn. M.	8.03.1967	4	0	0	0
Lynn. T.	2.01.1977	23 (12)	9	2	31
Lyon.	3.05.1941	6	0	0	0
Lyon. H.	17.11.1928	121	25	0	75
Lytten. P.	15.03.1970	1	0	0	0
Macklin. A.	16.08.1968	314 (14)	121	34	431
Macklin. J.	24.03.1962	142 (4)	13	2	43
Madden. B.	17.01.1948	64	19	18	93
Madley. I.	8.04.1981	2 (6)	1	0	3
Mahoney. E.	14.09.1895	60	6	0	18
Major. J.F.	22.10.1904	135	19	0	57
Mallinson. W.	14.04.1985	19	5	0	20
Maloney. J.	2.10.1965	224 (1)	38	675	1464
Mansell. W.	7.09.1895	78	8	0	24
Markham.	21.12.1940	2	0	0	0
Markham. H.	20.10.1951	182	39	0	117
Markham. J.W.	23.04.1910	4	0	0	0
Marland. H.	2.09.1905	14	0	0	0
Marshall. A.	10.09.1972	9 (8)	1	3	9
Marshall. D.	6.02.1977	41 (1)	3	86	181
Marson. L. (Wakefield)	12.12.1942	1	0	0	0
Maskill. A.	16.10.1977	8 (3)	0	0	0
Mason.	21.04.1974	1	0	0	0
Mason. P.	8.10.1921	4	1	0	3
Mathers. G.E.	24.09.1932	40	2	0	6
Matterson. R.	11.09.1897	8	1	0	3
Matthews. G.	27.09.1958	139	65	0	195
M'Barki. H.	2.09.1987	13 (1)	1	0	4
Meek. R.	1.04.1899	10	8	0	24
Mennell. A.	14.09.1895	2	0	0	0
Mercer. W.	13.04.1914	4	3	0	9
Merry. A.J.	5.09.1912	35	4	0	12
Metcalf. W.	11.01.1930	114	22	0	66

Player	Debut Date	App.(sub)	Tries	Goals	Points
Michaels. R.	4.11.1973	8	3	0	24
Miller. A.	16.10.1926	9	2	0	6
Miller. Fred	7.09.1901	43	2	0	6
Miller. Freddie	18.04.1933	385	23	558	1185
Mills. H.	23.09.1939	52	16	1	50
Mills. J.	18.09.1920	16	6	0	18
Mills. R. (HKR)	20.11.1943	2	3	0	9
Mills. T.H.	8.02.1930	1	0	0	0
Mills. W.A.	1.02.1930	46	13	0	39
Milner. J.W.	9.11.1929	44	6	0	18
Milner. T.	25.03.1914	137	20	1	65
Mitchell. G.	7.02.1925	5	1	0	3
Moat. R.	4.04.1953	81	47	0	141
Monkhouse. R.	7.09.1940	21	1	0	3
Moor. D.	18.09.1965	2	0	0	0
Moore.	3.01.1942	1	0	0	0
Moore.	8.04.1950	2	0	0	0
Morgan. E.D.	27.08.1921	176	33	0	99
Morgan. I.	1.02.1902	37	4	0	12
Morgan. J.A.	6.04.1901	2	0	0	0
Morgan. J.S.	2.01.1926	11	4	5	22
Morgan. R.	20.08.1966	14	0	0	0
Morland. F.	22.04.1946	11	2	0	6
Morrell. W.J.	15.09.1934	55	1	0	3
Morrod. A.	4.03.1911	3	1	0	3
Morton.	18.04.1946	1	0	0	0
Morton. A.D.	20.03.1909	44	15	1	47
Mountain. C. (formerly C. Ali)	3.01.1959	24	8	0	24
Mowforth.	26.02.1944	1	0	0	0
Moxon. A.	25.12.1899	2	0	0	0
Muggleton. J.	21.10.1984	33 (4)	28	1Drop	113
Murphy. E. (Bramley)	12.09.1942	1	0	0	0
Murray. L.	10.10.1936	11	0	0	0
McAvoy. D.	5.10.1935	1	0	0	0
McCaffery. P.	8.11.1987	18 (2)	7	0	28
McCoid. C.	23.03.1986	16	5	0	20
McDonald. A.V.	13.04.1914	1	0	0	0
McGiever. T.	30.08.1924	12	2	0	6
McGlone. A.	16.11.1963	264 (4)	23	21	111
McGowan. K.	20.04.1962	19	1	0	3
McKenzie.	28.12.1946	1	0	0	0
McLane. J.	12.04.1972	1	0	0	0
McLauchlan. W.	30.11.1895	15	0	0	0
McManus. J.V.	3.10.1896	8	2	0	6
McNamara. E.	1.04.1967	- (1)	0	0	0
McVeigh. P.	5.10.1963	5	0	0	0
McWatt. W. (HKR)	6.03.1943	22	4	44	100
Napier. K.	5.09.1942	8	0	0	0
Neale. J.	9.11.1963	113 (1)	3	0	9
Newlove. J.	8.10.1978	67 (2)	14	0	42
Newlove. J.A.	23.03.1901	1	0	0	0
Newsome. F.	23.08.1919	50	3	0	9

Player	Debut Date	App.(sub)	Tries	Goals	Points
Ness. W. (HKR)	6.09.1941	68	24	2	76
Nicholson.	20.09.1941	6	0	0	0
Nicholson. D.	19.09.1959	12	5	0	15
Nicklin. B.	19.04.1948	14	0	6	12
Nimb. C.	13.10.1962	26	1	19	41
Noble. A.	30.11.1946	11	0	0	0
Noble. D.	11.11.1977	6 (1)	2	1	8
Nolan. E.T.	25.12.1912	22	4	0	12
Norfolk. C.	7.09.1986	1	0	0	0
Northern. G.	26.03.1949	19	2	3	12
Northrop. W.	3.09.1904	1	0	0	0
Norton. S.	29.01.1978	267 (17)	47	11Drop	157
Nowell.	18.12.1943	1	0	0	0
Nutland. D.J.	21.04.1951	6	2	0	6
O'Brien. S.	16.01.1965	75 (5)	8	0	24
O'Donnell. G.	28.08.1971	3	0	0	0
O'Hara. D.	27.09.1981	232	110	0	408
Oldham. J.P.	4.09.1913	95	13	0	39
O'Leary. P.	4.03.1950	20	7	1	23
Oliver. F.W.	30.01.1904	2	0	0	0
Oliver. G.	27.08.1921	99	1	0	3
Oliver. J.	27.10.1928	426	156	687	1842
Oliver. N.	11.09.1965	100 (5)	35	0	105
Orme.	24.12.1932	2	0	0	0
Osbourne. W.T.	20.10.1906	52	2	0	6
Oulton. H.	19.12.1976	3	1	10	23
Overton. E.	24.02.1934	57	14	0	42
Owbridge. M.	18.10.1967	66 (3)	6	2	22
Owen. J.	5.09.1907	41	1	0	3
Owens. K.	20.02.1965	14	3	0	9
Parker. (Warrington)	19.09.1942	2	0	0	0
Parkes. R.A.	23.03.1907	4	0	0	0
Parkinson. R.	28.01.1899	105	6	44	106
Parry. L.	2.11.1901	138	65	1	197
Patrick. I.	31.03.1985	3 (1)	1	0	4
Patrick. S.	28.08.1983	143	9	0	36
Pattinson.	5.09.1936	1	0	0	0
Payne. J.	11.12.1948	20	2	0	6
Peacham. G.	15.09.1979	23 (5)	4	2	16
Pearce. G.	21.09.1986	58 (2)	17	153+11Drop	385
Pearson. C.	19.04.1910	1	0	0	0
Pearson. G.	23.01.1965	44	3	0	9
Perrett. F.L.	10.04.1914	32	2	0	6
Phillipson. J.	17.12.1927	96	21	21	105
Pickerill. C.	10.12.1978	83 (3)	8	1Drop	25
Pickering. S.	3.04.1924	239	2	0	6
Pickersgill. W.	2.11.1963	3	0	0	0
Pinder. G.	16.04.1938	66	7	0	21
Plugge. A.	21.09.1895	41	0	0	0
Poole. B.	31.08.1946	72	8	1	26
Popplewell.	12.09.1896	1	0	0	0

Player	Debut Date	App.(sub)	Tries	Goals	Points
Portz. J.	17.03.1985	15 (5)	4	0	16
Portz. S.	24.03.1972	104 (7)	33	0	99
Pougher.	27.08.1932	1	0	0	0
Prendiville. P.	1.10.1978	210 (5)	98	113+1Drop	529
Price. R.	2.09.1987	7 (4)	1	0	4
Proctor. W.	16.02.1982	72 (42)	13	0	52
Puckering. J.	8.12.1962	4	0	0	0
Puckering. N.	21.08.1983	46 (24)	8	0	32
Pullen. W.H.	13.01.1906	16	4	0	12
Purcheon. G.R.	9.04.1909	1	0	0	0
Ramsden. J. (HKR)	4.10.1941	22	1	0	3
Ramsey. W.	16.02.1975	32 (2)	4	7+4Drop	30
Read. W.J.	26.12.1895	13	2	0	6
Reed.	25.08.1934	2	0	0	0
Regan. T.	25.10.1987	25	1	1Drop	5
Reynolds. M.	23.09.1961	5	2	0	6
Rhodes. J.H.	30.10.1897	1	0	0	0
Rhodes. R.	11.09.1897	190	10	1	32
Richardson.	22.04.1933	4	2	0	6
Richardson. L.	24.10.1953	12	1	0	3
Riches. W.	15.08.1953	74	14	0	42
Rippon. J.H.	20.04.1896	79	7	0	21
Ritson. J.	7.09.1901	84	16	0	48
Robinson.	24.02.1945	1	0	0	0
Robinson. A.	26.09.1903	1	0	0	0
Robinson. G.	8.02.1976	134 (7)	28	62	209
Robson. D.	1.11.1969	79 (11)	12	0	36
Robson. V.	10.03.1945	4	0	0	0
Rogers. E.	24.11.1906	501	103	533	1375
Rogers. G.	25.04.1903	130	34	1	104
Rose. P.	22.08.1982	87 (8)	12	0	41
Rosenberg. W.	9.12.1961	87	42	0	126
Rowe. B.	1.02.1964	29	0	0	0
Rushton. D.	27.04.1949	21	9	0	27
Ryan. B.	23.08.1947	84	59	0	177
Salmon. A.	27.03.1973	89 (38)	25	0	75
Salt. T.	17.09.1904	11	2	0	6
Sampson. M.	14.11.1964	2	0	0	0
Samuel. F.	11.10.1922	20	0	2	4
Sanders. L.	4.01.1947	33	12	0	36
Sanderson. R.	25.12.1899	1	0	0	0
Savage. T.	11.09.1897	42	1	1	5
Saville. B.	19.01.1957	87	32	4	104
Schofield. D.	5.04.1981	3	0	0	0
Schofield. E.J.	4.11.1911	26	11	0	33
Schofield. G.	21.08.1983	116 (6)	107	197+2Drop	824
Scott. F.	8.04.1950	2	0	0	0
Scott. M.	2.04.1949	459	43	3	135
Scruton. I.	24.03.1981	14	2	0	6
Sedgwick. F.	12.09.1903	7	0	0	0
Shakesby. A.	31.08.1946	31	4	0	12
Sharp.	30.08.1930	5	0	0	0

Player	Debut Date	App.(sub)	Tries	Goals	Points
Sharp. J.	10.11.1900	21	11	0	33
Sharp. Jon.	26.12.1984	38 (13)	11	0	44
Sharpe. L.(York)	5.09.1942	7	0	0	0
Shaw. E.	1.09.1906	5	0	0	0
Shaw. J.	25.12.1899	1	0	0	0
Shaw. R.	20.10.1972	5 (3)	2	0	6
Shaw. S.	21.11.1942	57	10	10	50
Sheard.	18.03.1933	38	19	0	57
Shield. E.C.	3.03.1920	25	0	0	0
Shields.	17.10.1945	4	0	0	0
Shillito. F.W.	26.01.1946	48	3	0	9
Short. M.G.	22.09.1927	131	6	0	18
Sillis. G.	8.10.1898	17	0	3	6
Sinclair. A.D.	31.08.1946	95	21	14	91
Skerrett. T.	17.08.1980	147 (7)	18	0	57
Smailes. E.	7.09.1940	26	8	2	28
Small.J.	19.09.1903	3	0	0	0
Smallwood. J.T.	30.12.1922	112	29	0	87
Smith.	4.10.1941	9	2	0	6
Smith. J.	12.01.1957	24	10	0	30
Smith. J.P.	16.11.1912	6	0	0	0
Smith. J.W.	2.10.1897	38	6	0	18
Smith. Jack	8.04.1939	3	0	0	0
Smith. M.	14.05.1960	21	0	0	0
Smith. W. (Bradford)	19.12.1942	2	0	0	0
Solal. P.	24.04.1983	19 (6)	8	0	31
Soulsby. R.	11.09.1897	1	0	0	0
Sowerby. J.	18.09.1897	27	3	0	9
Sowerby. J.	3.09.1932	54	10	0	30
Spamer. B.	6.10.1945	19	0	46	92
Spenceley. F.	7.09.1895	130	4	0	12
Spencer. W.	3.11.1928	1	2	0	6
Stainforth. G.	18.11.1950	6	0	0	0
Staples. J.W.	21.09.1953	1	0	0	0
Stark. C.	12.12.1964	2	0	5	10
Stead. W.	7.11.1931	202	26	5	88
Stenton. I.	28.01.1973	26 (1)	5	0	15
Stephenson. J.(HKR)	7.09.1940	12	2	0	6
Stephenson. M.	7.12.1975	21	14	0	42
Stephenson. R.	26.09.1921	2	0	0	0
Sterling. P.	4.12.1983	34	9	0	36
Stevenson. G.	23.01.1909	20	0	0	0
Stitt. T.	1.09.1900	58	3	0	9
Stocks. G.	1.02.1964	106 (2)	22	0	66
Storey. M.	4.11.1961	29	7	0	21
Storry.	20.03.1943	5	2	0	6
Stone. C.	20.08.1978	183 (5)	8	0	24
Stone. W.H.	18.10.1919	222	149	40	527
Stringer. (York)	19.12.1942	1	0	0	0
Suddaby. C.	9.05.1982	- (2)	0	0	0
Sullivan. B.	13.04.1962	62	22	0	66
Sullivan. C.	9.12.1961	347 (5)	250	0	750
Sullivan. J.	7.12.1946	69	27	0	81
Sutton. F.	7.01.1905	2	0	0	0

Player	Debut Date	App.(sub)	Tries	Goals	Points
Sutton. M.	3.09.1977	42 (16)	3	0	9
Sutton. T.	14.03.1959	17	2	0	6
Sutton. T.H.	3.11.1928	5	0	0	0
Sweeting. S.	17.03.1945	27	1	0	3
Swinbank. J.A.	25.01.1908	5	0	0	0
Sykes. C.	15.09.1956	295 (2)	54	61	284
Sykes. E.	15.10.1910	17	4	1	14
Tanner. J.	20.11.1897	80	24	1	74
Tate. N.	13.12.1919	1	1	0	3
Tattersfield. E.	12.10.1946	5	0	0	0
Taylor. H.	25.09.1920	5	0	0	0
Taylor. J.	19.01.1929	1	0	0	0
Taylor. Joe.	8.10.1921	5	0	0	0
Taylor. R. (Dick)	25.09.1909	174	13	0	39
Taylor. R. (Bob)	31.01.1920	308	164	0	492
Taylor. R.	7.09.1940	50	10	51	132
Taylor. T.	2.11.1911	3	0	0	0
Taylor. W.H. (Harry)	1.01.1898	364	9	5	37
Teall. W.	26.12.1931	81	5	21	57
Thacker. L.	2.09.1933	282	43	0	129
Thames.	5.09.1931	17	0	0	0
Thomas. E.	26.10.1935	1	1	0	3
Thompson.	24.11.1945	2	0	0	0
Thompson. F.H.	13.03.1930	101	0	0	0
Thompson. H.	14.09.1895	32	1	22+2 Pen. +1Drop	79
Thompson. J.T.	3.09.1898	154	30	25	140
Thornton. W.	4.12.1926	1	0	0	0
Tidy. (HKR)	11.09.1943	4	0	0	0
Tindall. J.	23.09.1939	139	18	0	54
Tindall. K.	16.01.1972	213 (27)	34	0	102
Todd. G.	2.10.1920	22	5	0	15
Tomlinson. A.	21.03.1984	36 (5)	5	0	20
Tomlinson. T.	21.03.1896	2	0	0	0
Tomlinson. W.	23.03.1901	1	0	0	0
Tommerup. K.	15.12.1972	2	1	0	3
Topliss. D.	16.08.1981	113 (7)	56	2Drop	189
Townend. C.	7.09.1895	70	6	0	18
Townend. J.	7.09.1895	142	58	1+1Drop	180
Trelore. J.	2.09.1950	4	1	0	3
Tripp. A.	15.11.1952	70	10	0	30
Trotter. N.	5.03.1966	155 (34)	15	0	45
Troupe. J.	22.01.1898	11	1	0	3
Trowell. R.	21.10.1899	11	1	0	3
Turner. C.	26.03.1949	285	71	17	247
Turner. G.	15.01.1978	36	18	2	58
Vass. S.	4.12.1983	47 (6)	14	0	56
Voyce. G.	19.02.1898	86	11	0	33
Wade. J.	26.10.1901	63	3	2	13
Wainman. S.	17.04.1985	2	1	0	4

Player	Debut Date	App.(sub)	Tries	Goals	Points
Walford. L.	8.12.1906	10	6	0	18
Walker.	4.04.1942	2	0	0	0
Walker. M.	8.04.1972	50 (7)	7	0	21
Walker. W.	30.11.1901	2	0	0	0
Wallace. H.	1.09.1906	164	40	54	228
Walters. E.	25.11.1950	19	5	0	15
Walters. G.	30.09.1979	45 (2)	19	0	57
Walters. R.	19.04.1960	47	2	0	6
Waltham. B.	27.08.1973	9 (8)	1	0	3
Walton. H.	3.09.1908	55	13	0	39
Wanklyn. E.	27.09.1958	13	5	0	15
Wardell. A.	12.11.1972	105 (11)	6	2	22
Warters. P.	29.03.1958	2	0	0	0
Watkinson. J.	20.09.1952	51	7	23	67
Watson. E.	25.10.1919	4	1	0	3
Watt. G.	25.10.1947	89	9	1	29
Watts. I.	27.10.1945	413	214	5	652
Wear. H.	3.09.1904	2	0	0	0
Webster. H.	5.10.1912	16	0	0	0
Welham. P.	16.12.1984	29 (16)	7	0	28
Wellock.	1.12.1906	1	0	0	0
Wheeler. J.	19.01.1901	11	0	0	0
White. G.(HKR)	5.09.1942	1	0	0	0
Whitehead. T.	27.01.1962	44	0	0	0
Whiteley. J.W.	23.12.1950	417	156	2	472
Whiteley. P.	5.10.1957	88	17	0	51
Whittaker.	28.04.1934	8	1	0	3
Whitty. S.	27.12.1919	280	69	0	207
Wilby. T.	28.10.1979	56 (20)	11	0	34
Wiles. H.	21.09.1895	167	13	1	41
Wileman. R.	2.09.1979	87	23	0	70
Wileman. S.	23.10.1909	9	0	0	0
Williams. G.	1.10.1972	15 (2)	5	0	15
Williams. J.P.	25.01.1902	3	0	0	0
Williams. J.	8.03.1941	7	1	1	5
Willingham. P.	31.03.1985	1	0	0	0
Willoughby. M.	20.10.1972	1	0	0	0
Wilkinson. C.	1.10.1932	79	4	0	12
Wilkinson. H.	26.08.1939	74	0	0	0
Wilkinson. T.	11.01.1896	40	8	0	24
Wilson. I.	19.03.1978	17 (8)	7	0	21
Wilson. J.	5.09.1896	11	0	0	0
Wilson. J.	3.12.1955	16	4	0	12
Wilson. S.	8.12.1934	113	47	0	141
Wilson. W.	22.02.1941	11	3	0	9
Wilson. W.J.	27.01.1900	5	0	0	0
Windley. P.	8.04.1985	46 (9)	9	0	36
Winfield.	30.10.1943	22	0	0	0
Winsor. F.	10.03.1928	116	24	0	72
Wood.	31.01.1931	15	0	0	0
Wood. F.	21.11.1903	4	0	0	0
Woodcock. J.	7.11.1908	1	0	0	0
Woodhead. H.	1.09.1900	26	3	2	13
Woods. P.	23.09.1979	56	8	31+3Drop	89

Player	Debut Date	App.(sub)	Tries	Goals	Points
Worthy. M.	8.09.1945	10	3	0	9
Wray. E.	2.10.1937	47	3	0	9
Wray. G.E.	18.04.1930	3	0	0	0
Wright. D.	7.09.1895	8	0	0	0
Wyburn. J.E.	3.09.1914	162	26	0	78
Yewlett. M.	7.09.1911	3	0	0	0
Young. P.	1.01.1978	7 (3)	1	0	3

REPRESENTATIVE APPEARANCES

The following lists indicate the representative appearances by Hull FC. players to the end of 1987-88 season.

GREAT BRITAIN (formerly NORTHERN UNION)

(This section includes all Test Matches and World Cup encounters. Games against France were not accorded Test Match status until 1957. Opponents are indicated by: A = Australia: F = France: NZ = New Zealand: P = Papua. Substitute appearances are indicated by a small letter.)

Player	Tests(sub)	Opponents	Scores
Batten. W.	1	A.1921	
Bowman. H.	8	NZ.1924(2); NZ.1926(2); A.1928(2) NZ.1928; A.1929	1 Try
Boylen. F.	1	A.1908	
Coverdale. R.	4	A.1954; F.1954(2); NZ.1954	
Crane. M.	1	A.1982	
Crooks. L.	11 (2)	A.1982(2); A.1984(2); f.1984 NZ.1985; nz 1985; F.1986(2); A.1986(3); F.1987	16 Goals 1 Drop Goal
Dannatt. A.	2	F.1985(2)	
Divorty. G.	2	F.1985(2)	1Try: 1Goal
Drake. J.	1	F.1960	
Drake. W.	1	F.1962	
Evans. S.	2	A.1982(2)	1 Try
Farrar. V.	1	A.1982	
Gemmell. R.	2	F.1986; F.1969	2 Tries
Gwynne. T.E.	3	A.1928; NZ.1928; A.1929	
Harris. T	25	NZ.1954(2); A.1956(3); F.1957(6); A.1957; A.1958(3); NZ.1958; F.1958; A.1959(3); F.1959(2); F.1960(2); NZ.1960	2 Tries
Harrison. M.	7	F.1967(2); NZ.1971(2); F.1972(2); A.1973	
Holder. W.	1	NZ.1907	
Keegan. A.	9	A.1966(2); A.1967(3); F.1967(2); F.1968; F.1969	1 Try 5 Goals
Morgan. E.	2	A.1921(2)	
Norton. S.	9	A.1978(3); A.1979(2); NZ.1980; F.1981(2); A.1982	

108

Player	Tests(sub)	Opponents	Scores
Proctor. W.	- (1)	p.1984	
Rose. P.	1	A.1982	
Schofield. G.	15	F.1984: A.1984(3); NZ.1984; NZ.1985(3)	12 Tries
		F.1986(2); A.1986(3); F.1987(2);	2 Goals
			1 Drop Goal
Skerrett. T.	6	NZ.1980(2); F.1981(2); A.1982(2)	
Stone. W.	8	A.1920(3); NZ.1920(3); A.1921(2)	8 Tries; 1 Goal
Sullivan. C.	17	F.1967; A.1968; F.1968; NZ.1968;	
		A.1970; NZ.1971(3); F.1972(2);	13 Tries
		A.1972(2); F.1972; NZ.1972; A.1973(3)	
Taylor.W.H.	3	NZ.1907(3)	
Taylor. R.(Bob)	2	A.1921; NZ.1926	2 Tries
Topliss. D.	1	A.1982	
Whiteley. J.	15	A.1957; A.1958(3); NZ.1958; A.1959(2);	
		F.1959(2); F.1960(2); NZ.1960; NZ.1961(2);	2 Tries
		F.1962(2)	

HULL F.C. PLAYERS 'DOWN UNDER'

In 1910, the Northern Union, after lengthy negotiation with the Australian Authorities, decided to send a Touring team to Australia and New Zealand following the visits of their teams to this country in 1907-08 and 1908-09. Since then, and only interrupted by War, tours have taken place usually at 4-yearly intervals. These have also been supplemented by World Cup Touring Teams. With few exceptions, Hull F.C. has been represented on most Tours. The following is an analysis of appearances and scoring of Hull players on the Tours.

	App.(sub)	Tries	Goals	Points
1910				
Boylen. F.	7	1	5	13
1914				
Francis. A.	3	6	0	18
1920				
Stone. W.J.	17	24	1	74
1924				
Bowman. H.	14	8	0	24
Whitty. S.	14	5	0	15
(Mr. J.H. Dannatt (Hull) was a Manager of the Tour)				
1928				
Bowman. H.	14	2	0	6
Gwynne. T.E.	11	7	0	21
1936				
Ellerington. H.	11	6	0	18
1954				
Harris. P.T.	14	3	0	9
1957 (World Cup Tour)				
Harris. P.T.	8	1	0	3
Whiteley. J.	6	3	0	9
1958				
Harris. P.T.	14	7	0	21
Whiteley. J.	13	8	0	24

	App.(sub)	Tries	Goals	Points
1966				
Keegan. A.	15	1	62	127
1968 (World Cup Tour)				
Sullivan. C.	5 (1)	11	0	33
1970				
Sullivan. C.	8	3	0	9
(J.W. Whiteley (Hull)was the Manager/Coach)				
1979				
Norton. S.	9	0	0	0
Stone. C.	12	0	0	0
(Mr. R. Gemmell (Hull) was a Manager of the Tour)				
1984				
Crooks. L.	9 (1)	1	3	10
Proctor. W.	9 (2)	6	0	24
Schofield. G.	9 (2)	7	6	40
(Mr. R. Gemmell (Hull) was a Manager of the Tour)				

N.B. Test Match/World Cup appearances are included in the above.

ENGLAND	App.(sub)	Tries	Goals	Points
Batten. W.	4			
Booth. C. (Snr)	3			
Bowers. A.	2	2		6
Bowman. H.	4			
Brogden. S.	4	1		3
Boylen. F.	3			
Clarkson. E.	3			
Drake. W.	1			
Ellerington. H.	2			
Herbert. E.	2	1		3
Holder. W.	1			
Johnson. T.	1			
Keegan. A.	2			
Markham. H.	1			
Norton. S.	3	1		3
Oliver. J.	3	2		6
Schofield. G.	1			
Scott. M.	2			
Stone. W.	6	6	1	20
Taylor. H.	2			
Taylor. R.	6	7		21
Thacker. L.	4	1		3
Tindall. K.	1			
Wallace. H.	1			
Whiteley. J.	1			

WALES	App.(sub)	Tries	Goals	Points
Caswell. E.	3	1		3
Danter. T.	4			
Evans. H.	1			
Francis. A.	1	1		3
Gwynne. T.E.	1			

WALES

	App.(sub)	Tries	Goals	Points
Harris. P.T.	9	2		6
Merry. J.A.	1			
Morgan. E.	5	2		6
Oliver. W.	2			
Prendiville. P.	4 (2)			
Skerrett. T.	3			
Sullivan. C.	5	4		12
Turner. G.	1			
Walters G.	2			
Woods. P.	3		3	6

GREAT BRITAIN UNDER 24/21

	App.(sub)	Tries	Goals	Points
Crampton. J.	4	1		3
Crooks. L.	3			
Dannatt. A.	6			
Divorty. G.	6	3		12
Eastwood. P.	2	2		8
Evans. S.	1	1		3
Harrison. M.	1			
Maloney. J.	1			
McGlone. A.	1			
Proctor. W.	1 (1)			
Puckering. N.	4	3		12
Schofield. G.	2 (2)	1		4
Sullivan. C.	1			

NORTHERN RUGBY LEAGUE/R.L.XIII

	App.(sub)	Tries	Goals	Points
Allen. A.E.	1	1		3
Booth. C. (Snr)	5	1		3
Clarkson. E.	2			
Corner. R.	1	1		3
Dawson. J.R.P.	3	1		3
Drake. J.	1			
Ellerington. H.	5	3		9
Fifield. C.R.	1			
Harris. P.T.	1			
Hattersley. S.	1	1		3
Scott. M.	1			
Thacker. L.	5	1		3

OTHER NATIONALITIES

	App.(sub)	Tries	Goals	Points
Freear. A.E.	1			
Jackson. D.	5			
Payne. J.	1			

REST OF LEAGUE XIII

	App.(sub)	Tries	Goals	Points
Harris. P.T.	1			
Markham. H.	1			

REST OF WORLD XIII

	App.(sub)	Tries	Goals	Points
Whiteley. J.	1			

111

BRITISH XIII	App.(sub)	Tries	Goals	Points
Harris. P.T.	6	1		3
Whiteley. J.	4	3		9

YORKSHIRE	App.(sub)	Tries	Goals	Points
Barlow G.	1			
Barlow. L.	2			
Bateman. G.W.	4	4		12
Bateson. A.E.	3	1	5	13
Batten. W.	6	2		6
Booth. C. (Snr)	5			
Bowers. A.	2			
Bowman. H.	13	6		18
Bowman. K.	4	1		3
Boxall. K.	3	2		6
Boylen. F.	4			
Brogden. S.	3			
Burchall. J.	1			
Carroll. W.	2			
Connell. G.	1			
Coverdale. R.	3	1		3
Crooks. L.	1			
Dale. W.	1			
Dannatt. A.	- (1)			
Davidson. C.	2	1		3
Dawson. J.R.P.	1			
Day. T.	2			
Devereaux. J.	1	2		6
Donkin. L.	3			
Driscoll. J.	2			
Eastwood. P.	1			
Ellerington. H.	1			
Farrar. V.	- (2)			
Firth. H.	- (1)			
Frank. D.	4	1		3
Garrett. H.	1			
Hambling. B.	1			
Hambrecht. A.	1			
Hancock. B.	1 (2)			
Harrison. M.	5			
Herbert. E.	2	1		3
Herridge. T.	6			
Holdstock. A.	1			
Holdsworth. J.	2			
Jacques. W.	1			
Jenney. E.	4		2	4
Keegan. A.	13	3	7	23
Kennedy. J.E.	1		1	2
Kilburn. G.	3			
Lawrence. E.	2			
Lempriere. C.C.	1			
Lloyd. G.	1		2	4
Macklin. J.	1		1	2
Major. J.	4			
Markham. H.	2			

YORKSHIRE

	App.(sub)	Tries	Goals	Points
Miller. Fred.	2		5	10
Milner. T.	1	1		3
Morgan. E.	1			
Norton. S.	5			
Parkinson. R.	1			
Rhodes. R.	1			
Riches. W.	3			
Ritson. J.	1			
Rogers. E.	2			
Schofield. G.	1		1 Drop	1
Scott. M.	16	2		6
Skerrett. T.	3			
Stead. W.	2			
Stone. W.	1	1		3
Taylor.W.H.	19			
Thacker. L.	4			
Tindall. K.	3			
Todd. G.	1			
Wade. J.	1			
Wallace. H.	1			
Whiteley. J.	12	4		12
Whitty. S.	5			
Wilby. T.	- (1)			
Wileman. R.	1			

YORKSHIRE LEAGUE XIII

	App.(sub)	Tries	Goals	Points
Booth. C. (Snr)	1			
Mills. H.	1			

LANCASHIRE

	App.(sub)	Tries	Goals	Points
Clarkson. E.	1	1		3
Gemmell. R.	1	2		6
Taylor. R.(Bob)	4	3		9

CUMBERLAND

	App.(sub)	Tries	Goals	Points
Atkinson. H.	1			
Drake. J.	5	1		3
Drake. W.	10	1		3
Marland. H.	1			
Neale. J.	1			
Oliver. J.	27	11	12	57
Ritson. J.	2			
Watts. I.	12	3		9

NORTHUMBERLAND & DURHAM

	App.(sub)	Tries	Goals	Points
Lewis. G.H.	1			
Lewis. J.	1			
Parkinson. J.F.	1			
Ritson. J.	7	2		6
Thompson. J.	3			

GLAMORGAN	App.(sub)	Tries	Goals	Points
Davies. W.J.	1	1		3
Gwynne. T.E.	1	1		3

GLAMORGAN & MONMOUTHSHIRE	App.(sub)	Tries	Goals	Points
Caswell. E.	1			
Gwynne. T.E.	1			

MIDLANDS & SOUTH	App.(sub)	Tries	Goals	Points
Herridge. T.	1			

DOMINIONS XIII	App.(sub)	Tries	Goals	Points
Fifield. C.R.	1			

BRITISH EMPIRE XIII	App.(sub)	Tries	Goals	Points
Booth. C. (Snr)	1			
Thacker. L.	1			
Scott. M.	1	2		6

AUSTRALASIA	App.(sub)	Tries	Goals	Points
Payne. J.	1			

ARMY XIII	App.(sub)	Tries	Goals	Points
Dockar. W.	1			

NORTHERN COMMAND XIII	App.(sub)	Tries	Goals	Points
Brogden. S.	1	2		6

MISCELLANEOUS APPEARANCES

In the early days of the Northern Union, before the Championship Play-off was introduced. it was customary for the League Leaders (Champions) to play a side selected from the rest of the League. The following players took part in these games:-

W. Dale	1 appearance	W. Johnson	1 appearance
L. Donkin	1 appearance	W.H. Taylor	1 appearance
J. Driscoll	2 appearances		

YORKSHIRE COUNTY TRIAL MATCHES: (1895-1910)

Boylen. F.	2		Herridge. T.	3	(2 Tries)
Burchell. H.	2		Jacques. W.	3	(5 Goals)
Carroll. W.	2		Jenkins. C.	1	
Carvill. P.	2		Kilburn. G.	2	
Cook. J.	1	(1 Try)	Lempriere. C.C.	4	(2 Tries)
Dale. W.	2	(2 Tries: 1 Goal)	Low. C.	1	
Devereaux. J.	2		Major. J.	4	(4 Tries)
Donkin. L.	2		Parkinson. R.	3	

Driscoll. J.	2	(1 Try: 1 Goal)	Taylor. W.H.	7	(2 Goals)
Frank. D.	1		Thompson. J.	1	
Freear. A.E.	2		Wade. J.	1	
Gorman. F.	1		Wiles. H.	1	
Hall. W.	1				

TOUR TRIAL MATCHES:

1910:	Boylen. F.	(2)	1932:	Bateman. G.W.	(1)
	Herridge. T.	(2)		Bowman. H.	(1)
	Anderson. W.	(1)	1936:	Ellerington. H.	(1)
1914:	Rogers. E.	(1)		Miller. F.	(1)
1920:	Stone. W.	(1)	1954:	Scott. M.	(1)
	Kennedy. J.	(1)		Whiteley. J.	(1)
1924:	Stone. W.	(1)-1 Try		Harris. T.	(1)
	Whitty. S.	(2)-1 Try	1958:	Whiteley. J.	(1)
	Bowman. H.	(1)		Drake. W.	(1)
1928:	Gwynne. E.	(2)-1 Try		Bateson. P.	(1)-7 Goals
	Bowman. H.	(1)			
	Bateson. A.E.	(1)-2 Goals			

RECORD OF MATCHES PLAYED:

LEAGUE	Played	Won	Drawn	Lost	Points For	Against
Acton & Willesden	2	2	-	-	35	7
Barrow	44	31	3	10	826	496
Batley	144	88	4	52	2050	1195
Bradford Northern	165	95	7	63	2389	1615
Bramley	132	93	3	36	2505	1105
Brighouse Rangers	18	9	2	7	154	59
Broughton Rangers/						
Bell Vue Rangers	48	26	2	20	488	390
Blackpool Borough	16	15	-	1	366	123
Cardiff	2	2	-	-	54	13
Carlisle	2	2	-	-	32	6
Castleford	120	63	7	50	1721	1425
Coventry	4	4	-	-	74	14
Dewsbury	129	76	10	43	1965	1314
Doncaster	46	43	1	2	1349	313
Ebbw Vale	6	4	1	1	106	21
Featherstone Rovers	117	81	1	35	1871	1305
Fulham	4	2	-	2	93	62
Halifax	139	69	3	67	1508	1470
Heckmondwike	6	6	-	-	92	11
Holbeck	10	6	1	3	96	40
Huddersfield	143	72	5	66	1702	1920
Hull Kingston Rovers	154	76	10	68	1702	1574
Hunslet (incl.New Hunslet)	163	89	5	69	2061	1694
Huyton	18	12	2	4	307	195
(Liverpool City, Liverpool Stanley and Wigan Highfield)						
Keighley	129	90	4	35	2262	1037
Leeds	166	75	9	82	2016	2148
Leeds Parish Church	10	7	1	2	67	38

LEAGUE	Played	Won	Drawn	Lost	Points For	Against
Leigh	62	31	6	25	729	769
Liversedge	12	11	-	1	194	8
Manningham	12	4	1	7	91	83
Merthyr Tydfil	2	2	-	-	33	0
Mid-Rhondda	2	2	-	-	51	13
Newcastle	4	3	-	1	88	34
Oldham	96	36	1	59	1052	1231
Pontypridd	2	1	-	1	34	18
Rochdale Hornets	28	18	-	10	474	231
Runcorn	16	9	-	7	164	137
(This club played in the early years and should not be confused with the later club in the 1980's)						
St. Helens	73	28	5	40	930	1169
St. Helens Recreation	20	12	-	8	281	225
Salford	54	23	4	27	658	603
Stockport	2	1	-	1	15	8
Swinton	76	32	5	39	825	767
Tyldesley	2	-	-	2	0	21
Wakefield Trinity	154	82	6	66	1961	1798
Warrington	94	38	4	52	1142	1404
Whitehaven	20	14	1	5	463	165
Widnes	70	34	6	30	861	813
Wigan	95	36	2	57	939	1654
Workington Town	35	14	4	17	566	461
York	142	100	4	38	2340	1215
Total	3010	1669	130	1211	41,782	32,417

RUGBY LEAGUE CUP	Played	Won	Drawn	Lost	Points For	Against
Barrow	6	3	-	3	26	34
Batley	8	5	2	1	82	27
Bickershaw Hornets	1	1	-	-	44	10
Blackpool Borough	2	2	-	-	30	13
B.O.C.M. (Hull)	1	1	-	-	75	2
Bradford Northern	6	2	1	3	19	33
Bramley	8	7	-	1	132	25
Broughton Rangers/ Belle Vue Rangers	4	3	-	1	65	28
Cardiff City	1	1	-	-	34	6
Carlisle	1	1	-	-	52	6
Castleford	8	4	2	2	71	67
Dewsbury	7	2	-	5	71	100
Doncaster	2	2	-	-	61	21
Dudley Hill (Bradford)	1	1	-	-	38	10
Elland	1	1	-	-	86	0
Featherstone Rovers	7	5	1	1	104	46
Fulham	1	1	-	-	11	5
Halifax	17	10	1	6	165	112
Higginshaw	1	1	-	-	37	9
Huddersfield	6	2	-	4	31	54
Hull Kingston Rovers	11	6	-	5	102	94

RUGBY LEAGUE CUP	Played	Won	Drawn	Lost	Points For	Against
Hull Marlborough	1	1	-	-	45	0
Hunslet	6	1	-	5	37	52
(includes New Hunslet)						
Huyton	4	2	-	2	82	29
(incl. Liverpool City, Liverpool Stanley, Wigan Highfield)						
Keighley	4	3	-	1	80	31
Leeds	13	3	1	9	100	170
Leigh	4	2	-	2	29	27
Leigh Shamrocks	1	1	-	-	52	0
Mansfield Marksmen	1	1	-	-	38	7
Millom	3	3	-	-	61	10
Morecambe	1	1	-	-	8	0
Normanton	1	1	-	-	20	10
Oldham	7	4	-	3	55	103
Pemberton Rovers	1	1	-	-	27	3
Radcliffe	1	1	-	-	18	0
Rochdale Hornets	8	4	1	3	84	50
Runcorn	2	2	-	-	17	9
(This club played in the early years and should not be confused with the later club in the 1980's)						
St. Helens	7	2	-	5	58	86
St. Helens Recreation	2	1	-	1	11	20
Salford	8	6	-	2	114	98
Seaton (Cumberland)	1	1	-	-	24	2
Sheffield Eagles	1	1	-	-	26	6
Swinton	9	4	-	5	78	79
Wakefield Trinity	10	7	1	2	109	93
Walkden	1	1	-	-	9	0
Warrington	10	3	2	5	78	93
Wath Brow Hornets	1	1	-	-	52	0
Whitehaven	3	1	-	2	24	25
Widnes	13	7	2	4	133	111
Wigan	9	3	-	6	98	127
Workington Town	2	-	1	1	19	22
York	6	6	-	-	85	26
Total	241	136	15	90	3007	1991

YORKSHIRE CUP	Played	Won	Drawn	Lost	Points For	Against
Batley	9	8	-	1	148	62
Bradford Northern	8	5	-	3	104	81
Bramley	13	13	-	-	267	128
Castleford	12	5	3	4	154	127
Dewsbury	13	5	2	6	76	96
Doncaster	1	1	-	-	42	0
Featherstone Rovers	16	10	1	5	207	125
Halifax	15	6	1	8	159	166
Huddersfield	22	9	1	12	287	320
Hull Kingston Rovers	10	5	-	5	138	110
Hunslet	18	11	-	7	211	159
(incl. New Hunslet)						

YORKSHIRE CUP	Played	Won	Drawn	Lost	Points For	Against
Keighley	8	6	-	2	160	67
Leeds	22	11	2	9	291	257
Wakefield Trinity	17	4	1	12	151	243
York	10	5	-	5	168	94
Total	194	104	11	79	2563	2035

JOHN PLAYER TROPHY	Played	Won	Drawn	Lost	Points For	Against
Barrow	2	1	-	1	24	25
Blackpool Borough	1	1	-	-	48	22
Bradford Northern	6	3	1	2	83	53
Bramley	2	-	-	2	18	35
Castleford	2	2	-	-	31	9
Dewsbury	3	2	1	-	49	23
Doncaster	1	1	-	-	23	12
Featherstone Rovers	2	1	-	1	32	24
Fulham	1	1	-	-	36	14
Halifax	1	1	-	-	26	7
Hull Kingston Rovers	2	1	-	1	12	16
Hunslet	1	1	-	-	17	7
Keighley	2	1	-	1	52	28
Leeds	5	2	2	1	73	81
Leigh	2	1	-	1	31	24
Oldham	3	3	-	-	65	30
St. Helens	4	1	-	3	44	118
Salford	3	3	-	-	79	36
Swinton	1	1	-	-	44	0
Wakefield Trinity	2	1	-	1	27	29
Warrington	1	1	-	-	18	5
Whitehaven	1	1	-	-	13	0
Widnes	1	-	-	1	13	19
Wigan	1	-	-	1	11	12
Workington Town	1	1	-	-	42	6
York	1	1	-	-	11	10
Total	52	32	4	16	922	645

B.B.C.2 TROPHY	Played	Won	Drawn	Lost	Points For	Against
Barrow	1	1	-	-	6	0
Bramley	1	1	-	-	18	11
Castleford	2	-	-	2	15	25
Halifax	3	3	-	-	48	34
Huddersfield	2	2	-	-	49	9
Hull Kingston Rovers	3	1	-	2	29	33

B.B.C.2 TROPHY	Played	Won	Drawn	Lost	Points For	Against
Keighley	2	2	-	-	28	4
Leeds	4	2	-	2	46	71
Leigh	1	1	-	-	9	6
Oldham	1	1	-	-	6	0
Rochdale Hornets	2	-	-	2	12	44
St. Helens	3	-	-	3	28	63
Wakefield Trinity	3	1	1	1	33	34
Widnes	1	1	-	-	22	13
Wigan	1	-	-	1	5	24
Total	30	16	1	13	354	371

CHAMPIONSHIP/PREMIERSHIP PLAY-OFFs	Played	Won	Drawn	Lost	Points For	Against
Barrow	1	1	-	-	45	14
Bradford Northern	1	1	-	-	42	12
Castleford	4	1	-	3	41	68
Dewsbury	1	-	-	1	18	32
Halifax	3	2	-	1	57	51
Huddersfield	2	1	-	1	8	25
Hull Kingston Rovers	3	1	-	2	25	41
Leeds	2	2	-	-	30	5
Leigh	1	-	-	1	0	8
Oldham	3	2	-	1	58	44
St. Helens	2	1	-	1	28	38
Salford	1	-	-	1	4	11
Swinton	2	2	-	-	36	22
Wakefield Trinity	3	-	-	3	19	75
Warrington	5	3	-	2	84	60
Widnes	3	1	-	2	39	47
Wigan	6	1	-	5	52	149
Workington Town	2	2	-	-	34	6
York	2	1	-	1	51	35
Total	47	22	-	25	671	743

EUROPEAN CHAMPIONSHIP	Played	Won	Drawn	Lost	Points For	Against
Albi (France)	2	1	1	-	42	26
Carcassonne (France)	2	2	-	-	41	10

OTHER MATCHES	Played	Won	Drawn	Lost	Points For	Against
Australia	11	1	-	10	57	267
France XIII	2	1	-	1	47	46
New Zealand	8	1	-	7	87	162
Auckland	1	1	-	-	26	24
Total	26	7	1	18	300	535
Overall Total	3600	1986	162	1452	49,599	38,737

GAMES AGAINST TOURING TEAMS

During the period from 1956 to 1963, the visit to the City of Hull by the Australian or New Zealand Touring Team was marked by a game against a joint Hull F.C./Hull Kingston Rovers XIII. The following Hull players took part in the four games concerned.

Barnwell. K.	(1)	Hollindrake. T.	(2) 2 tries
Bateson. P.	(1) 3 goals	Keegan. A.	(1) 2 goals
Devonshire. T.	(1)	Markham. H.	(1)
Drake. J.	(2)	Matthews. G.	(1)
Drake. W.	(3)	Moat. R.	(1)
Finn. T.	(2)	Scott. M.	(2)
Gittoes. K.	(1) 1 Try	Sykes. C.	(2)
Harris. T.	(3)	Turner. C.	(1)
		Whiteley. J.	(1)

	Played	Won	Drawn	Lost	Points For	Against
Australia	3	-	-	3	33	89
New Zealand	1	1	-	-	17	6

CLUB HONOURS

Rugby League Champions:-1919-20; 1920-21; 1935-36; 1955-56; 1957-58; 1982-83;
 (Runners-up):- 1956-57; 1981-82; 1983-84
Rugby League Second Division Champions:- 1976-77; 1978-79
Rugby League Challenge Cup: Winners:- 1913-14; 1981-82;
 (Runners-up):- 1907-08; 1908-09; 1909-10; 1921-22; 1922-23; 1958-59;
 1959-60; 1979-80; 1982-83; 1984-85
John Player Trophy Winners:- 1981-82;
 (Runners-up):- 1975-76; 1984-85
B.B.C.2 Floodlit Trophy: Winners:- 1979-80
Premiership Trophy: (Runners-up):- 1980-81; 1981-82; 1982-83
Yorkshire County Challenge Cup Winners:- 1923-24; 1969-70; 1982-83; 1983-84;
 1984-85;
 (Runners-up):- 1912-13; 1914-15; 1920-21; 1927-28; 1938-39; 1946-47;
 1953-54; 1954-55; 1955-56; 1959-60; 1967-68; 1986-87
Yorkshire League Champions:- 1918-19; 1922-23; 1926-27; 1935-36;
 (Runners-up):- 1913-14; 1919-20; 1920-21; 1934-35; 1940-41; 1953-54;
 1955-56; 1956-57; 1957-58; 1959-60
European Champions:- 1956-57

REPRESENTATIVE MATCHES AT THE 'BOULEVARD'

Date	Team	Score		Opponent	Score
07 Nov. 1896	Yorkshire	17	v	Cheshire	10
15 Dec. 1900	Yorkshire	10	v	Cumberland	5
25 Jan. 1902	Yorkshire	9	v	Durham/N'thumberland	0
15 Feb. 1902	Yorkshire	13	v	Lancashire	8
13 Oct. 1902	Yorks. Probables	10	v	Yorks. Possibles	3
24 Nov. 1904	Yorkshire	12	v	Cheshire	0
04 Nov. 1905	Yorkshire	0	v	Lancashire	8
10 Oct. 1906	(Y.C.Trial) Whites	30	v	Stripes	22
05 Nov. 1908	Yorkshire	11	v	Australia	24
04 Nov. 1909	Yorkshire	27	v	Lancashire	14
21 Oct. 1920	Yorkshire	18	v	Lancashire	3
05 Nov. 1921	Northern Union	2	v	Australia	16
13 Nov. 1926	Great Britain	21	v	New Zealand	11
10 Oct. 1942	Rugby League XIII	10	v	Northern Command	14
26 Sep. 1949	Yorkshire	21	v	Cumberland	8
03 Nov. 1951	Other Nationalities	17	v	France	14
28 Apr. 1953	Yorkshire	16	v	Lancashire	8
26 Sep. 1956	Yorkshire	21	v	Lancashire	35
11 Sep. 1957	Yorkshire	27	v	Cumberland	18
16 Sep. 1959	Yorkshire	13	v	Cumberland	26
23 Sep. 1964	Yorkshire	33	v	Lancashire	10
25 Oct. 1970	New Zealand	16	v	France	15
12 Nov. 1977	Great Britain (Under 24)	17	v	France (under 24)	9
20 Sep. 1978	Yorkshire	37	v	Cumbria	9
06 Dec. 1981	Great Britain	37	v	France	0
06 Mar. 1983	Great Britain	17	v	France	5

HIGH SCORING GAMES INVOLVING HULL F.C.

1. Hull having scored 50 or more points:

01 Apr. 1899	Hull	86	v	Elland	0
29 Jan. 1921	Hull	80	v	Keighley	11
07 Apr. 1921	Hull	79	v	Rochdale	2
21 Feb. 1920	Hull	75	v	BOCM (Hull)	2
22 Mar. 1919	Hull	69	v	York	0
15 Jan. 1921	Hull	69	v	Wakefield	11
25 Mar. 1984	Hull	66	v	Wakefield	12
28 Dec. 1914	Hull	65	v	Bradford	0
20 Apr. 1985	Workington	18	v	Hull	64
16 Mar. 1907	Hull	63	v	Liverpool C.	2
04 Feb. 1933	Hull	63	v	Bradford	3
05 Oct. 1957	Hull	62	v	Dewsbury	5
05 Oct. 1919	Hull	62	v	Hunslet	7
06 Mar. 1937	Hull	61	v	Bramley	7
07 May. 1955	Hull	61	v	Doncaster	7
10 Sep. 1978	Hull	61	v	Oldham	10
03 Jan. 1920	Hull	60	v	Batley	3
18 Sep. 1920	Hull	60	v	Bradford	4
26 Oct. 1957	Hull	59	v	Barrow	5
21 Sep. 1957	Hull	58	v	Bramley	2
30 Oct. 1983	Hull	58	v	Salford	6
21 Apr. 1985	Hull	58	v	Hunslet	6
20 Feb. 1960	Hull	58	v	Keighley	15
04 Apr. 1925	Hull	57	v	Bradford	6
15 Apr. 1968	Doncaster	6	v	Hull	57
12 Sep. 1976	Hull	57	v	Doncaster	7
09 Nov. 1957	Hull	56	v	Doncaster	2
29 Oct. 1955	Hull	56	v	Blackpool	13
26 Apr. 1955	Hull	55	v	Dewsbury	5
23 Apr. 1984	Hull	54	v	Whitehaven	0
22 Apr. 1979	Hull	54	v	Whitehaven	3
01 Feb. 1908	Hull	54	v	Bramley	5
02 Sep. 1987	Hull	54	v	Huddersfield	8
22 Sep. 1985	Hull	54	v	Oldham	12
13 Oct. 1926	Hull	54	v	Bradford	17
19 Sep. 1959	Hull	53	v	Doncaster	8
17 Mar. 1900	Hull	52	v	Wath Brow	0
04 Mar. 1905	Hull	52	v	Leigh Shamrocks	0
07 Apr. 1958	Castleford	2	v	Hull	52
16 Aug. 1958	Hull	52	v	Doncaster	6
14 Feb. 1985	Hull	52	v	Carlisle	6
12 Dec. 1931	Hull	52	v	Keighley	15
17 Apr. 1915	Hull	51	v	Wakefield	3
17 Jan. 1914	Hull	51	v	Warrington	8

2. Hull having had 50 or more points scored against them:

17 Feb. 1988	St. Helens	64	v	Hull	2
11 Dec. 1985	St. Helens	57	v	Hull	14
22 Apr. 1919	Dewsbury	56	v	Hull	0
12 Oct. 1957	Wigan	56	v	Hull	8
15 Nov. 1924	Huddersfield	53	v	Hull	7
23 Apr. 1973	Wakefield	52	v	Hull	0
16 Oct. 1977	St. Helens	52	v	Hull	14

19 Jan. 1907	Oldham	51	v	Hull	7
26 Apr. 1973	Bradford	51	v	Hull	18
23 Nov. 1986	St. Helens	50	v	Hull	10

HEAVIEST DEFEATS AT THE BOULEVARD

16 Nov. 1986	Hull	0	v	Australia	48
29 Mar. 1987	Hull	12	v	Warrington	46
04 Apr. 1964	Hull	12	v	Wigan	38
25 Oct. 1987	Hull	16	v	Castleford	37
15 Dec. 1972	Hull	8	v	Warrington	36
25 Sep. 1954	Hull	18	v	Leeds	36
26 Oct. 1929	Hull	2	v	Australia	35
27 Aug. 1932	Hull	18	v	Oldham	35
24 Nov. 1962	Hull	0	v	Wigan	34
29 Oct. 1978	Hull	2	v	Australia	34
01 Sep. 1985	Hull	10	v	Widnes	33
17 Nov. 1985	Hull	10	v	New Zealand	33
20 Sep. 1987	Hull	18	v	Widnes	33

CAREER SCORING RECORDS

TRIES		GOALS		POINTS	
250:	C.Sullivan	687:	J.Oliver	1842:	J.Oliver
214:	I.Watts	675:	J.Maloney	1464:	J.Maloney
166:	A.Francis	628:	C.Hutton	1375:	E.Rogers
164:	R.Taylor	558:	F.Miller	1325:	C.Hutton
156:	J.Whiteley	542:	P.Bateson	1250:	J.Kennedy
152:	J.Oliver	533:	E.Rogers	1182:	F.Miller
149:	W.Stone	523:	J.Kennedy	1099:	P.Bateson
131:	T.Finn	400:	L.Crooks	947:	L.Crooks
123:	G.W.Bateman	367:	G.Lloyd	824:	G.Schofield
123:	T.Devonshire	318:	A.Keegan	793:	G.Lloyd
121:	A.Macklin			729:	A.Keegan
110:	D.O'Hara			712:	K.Boxall
107:	T.E.Gwynne			701:	A.E.Bateson
107:	B.Hancock			652:	I.Watts
107:	G.Schofield			595:	T.Hart
103:	E.Rogers			563:	C.Davidson
101:	J.Devereaux			529:	P.Prendiville
101:	W.Drake			527:	W.Stone
				502:	A.Francis

SEASON SCORING RECORDS

TRIES			GOALS			POINTS		
52:	J.Harrison	1914-15	170:	G.Lloyd	1978-79	369:	G.Lloyd	1978-79
38:	A.Francis	1919-20	166:	C.Hutton	1956-57	335:	C.Hutton	1956-57
38:	W.Stone	1920-21	161:	P.Bateson	1959-60	328:	P.Bateson	1959-60
37:	G.Schofield	1983-84	140:	C.Hutton	1953-54	301:	G.Schofield	1984-85
33:	K.Bowman	1953-54	133:	C.Hutton	1955-56	295:	C.Hutton	1953-54
33:	C.Sullivan	1970-71	131:	P.Bateson	1957-58	272:	C.Hutton	1955-56
32:	I.Watts	1953-54	123:	J.Maloney	1966-67	267:	J.Maloney	1966-67
32:	R.Taylor	1925-26	121:	J.Maloney	1967-68	265:	P.Bateson	1957-58
30:	G.W.Bateman	1930-31	118:	L.Crooks	1981-82	264:	J.Kennedy	1920-21
30:	I.Watts	1956-57	115:	L.Crooks	1982-83	262:	G.Schofield	1983-84
30:	C.Sullivan	1971-72	111:	G.Pearce	1987-88	261:	L.Crooks	1982-83
			110:	C.Hutton	1954-55	257:	J.Maloney	1967-68
			110:	J.Maloney	1968-69	254:	L.Crooks	1981-82

MATCH SCORING RECORDS

TRIES

7:	C.Sullivan	15.4.68
6:	J.Harrison	28.12.14
6:	J.Harrison	17.4.15
6:	A.Francis	21.2.20
6:	J.Holdsworth	18.9.20
6:	R.Taylor	15.1.21
6:	H.Garrett	14.4.22
5:	C.C.Lempriere	7.1.1899
5:	J.Driscoll	1.4.1899
5:	A.Francis	22.3.19
5:	W.Stone	16.4.21
5:	B.Ryan	17.9.49
5:	I.Watts	5.9.59
5:	B.Sullivan	22.1.64
5:	P.Hunter	19.4.76

GOALS

14:	J.Kennedy	7.4.21
14:	G.Lloyd	10.9.78
13:	W.Jacques	1.4.1899
12:	J.Kennedy	21.2.20
12:	J.Kennedy	15.1.21
12:	J.Kennedy	29.1.21
11:	F.J.Goodfellow	4.3.05
11:	C.Hutton	7.5.55
11:	P.Bateson	20.2.60

POINTS

36:	J.Kennedy	29.1.21
31:	G.Lloyd	10.9.78
29:	W.Jacques	1.4.1899
28:	J.Kennedy	7.4.21
27:	J.Kennedy	3.1.20
27:	J.Kennedy	15.1.21
26:	J.Oliver	6.4.35
25:	C.Hutton	7.5.55
24:	J.Kennedy	21.2.20
24:	J.Oliver	4.2.33
24:	P.Bateson	22.10.60

APPEARANCES IN CAREER FOR HULL F.C.

501:	E. Rogers	374:	T. Finn
459:	M. Scott	363 + 1 Sub:	A. Keegan
451:	H. Bowman	364:	W.H. Taylor
443:	T. Harris	347 + 5 Sub:	C. Sullivan
426:	J. Oliver	336:	C. Booth (Snr)
417:	J. Whiteley	325 + 9 Sub:	T. Devonshire
413:	I. Watts	324 + 35 Sub:	M. Crane
401:	E. Caswell	318 + 3 Sub:	M. Harrison
396 + 15 Sub:	B Hancock	314 + 14 Sub:	A. Macklin
385:	F. Miller	308:	R. (Bob) Taylor
379:	T. Herridge		

CONSECUTIVE CLUB APPEARANCES

101:	M.G. Short	(20.10.27 to 23.11.29)
101:	F. Miller	(05.04.34 to 17.09.36)
83:	A. Keegan	(24.04.64 to 30.04.66)
76:	W. Teall	(26.12.31 to 25.10.33)
75:	W. Mansell	(07.09.1895 to 04.09.1897)
75:	C. Hutton	(26.09.53 to 16.04.55)

CONSECUTIVE CLUB APPEARANCES AS TRY SCORERS

11:	J. Harrison	(03.09.14 to 31.10.14)
8:	E. Rogers	(04.03.11 to 15.04.11)
8:	E. Lawrence	(05.09.46 to 10.10.46)
8:	M. Crane	(26.12.75 to 08.02.76)
8:	J. Leuluai	(21.08.83 to 28.09.83)
8:	S. Evans	(20.11.83 to 11.01.84)

CONSECUTIVE CLUB APPEARANCES
AS GOAL SCORERS/POINT SCORERS

36:	J. Maloney	(04.02.67 to 02.12.67)
34:	J. Maloney	(23.03.69 to 12.11.69)
33:	C. Hutton	(03.10.53 to 28.08.54)
30:	P. Bateson	(19.12.59 to 20.08.60)
29:	G. Schofield	(25.2.84 to 09.12.84)
27:	J. Maloney	(10.02.68 to 14.12.68)
26:	G. Lloyd	(12.11.78 to 19.08.79)
24:	J. Maloney	(20.08.66 to 14.01.67)

PREVIOUS BOOKS BY MICHAEL ULYATT

FOUR HULL TRAGEDIES

Printed & Published by
J.S. Sellers (1971)

HULL RAILWAY CLERKS
CRICKET CLUB
A Centenary History 1873 - 1973

Printed & Published by
J.S. Sellers (1973)

FLYING SAIL
Humber Keels and Sloops

Bradley Publications (1974)

HUMBER SHIPPING
A Pictorial History
In conjunction with Edward Paget-Tomlinson

Dalesman Books (1979)

LIFE IN OLD HULL
A Photographic Recollection

Dalesman Books (1983)

HULL KINGSTON ROVERS
A Centenary History 1883 - 1983

Lockington Publishing (1983)

TRAWLERMEN OF HULL

Dalesman Books (1985)

OLD HULL REMEMBERED

Dalesman Books (1986)

BARTON-UPON-HUMBER
In old picture postcards

European Library (1986)